The Power To
HEAL

The Power To
HEAL

John Hagee .

First printing, November 1991.

Contents

Chapter *1*

I Believe in Miracles

This book is written for everyone who needs a miracle or knows someone who does. If you don't need a miracle right now, you will someday.

Sooner or later it will happen to you. The phone will ring and from the moment you pick up the receiver, your life will never be the same.

The voice on the other end of the line may be the doctor, saying, "I'm afraid it's cancer, and there's nothing we can do."

The voice on the other end of the line may be the police officer, saying, "There's been a bad accident. You'd better come quickly."

The message can come a hundred different ways for a thousand different reasons, but the bottom line is the same: without a miracle, you, a member of your family, or a dear friend will die.

Miracles happen every day to those who know how to release the power of God through faith, according to his word. Regardless of your denomination, your doctrine or your doubting disposition—when life hangs in the balance, you will want a miracle.

If you are in need of a miracle right now, I have great news for you! The God of the Bible is a miracle-working God, and he invites you to release your faith and personally experience his miracle-working power in your life.

Why I believe in miracles

Why do I believe in miracles? First of all, I believe in miracles because I believe the word of God. The Bible is the greatest manuscript of miracles ever written. If you take the miracles from the pages of the Bible, all you have left is a sterile, lifeless manuscript. The Bible is the most powerful document ever written as authentication of the fact that our God is a miracle-working God and that miracles are for us today.

The Bible is not an ordinary book. It is not a good book—*Gone With The Wind* is a good book. The Bible is a living book. "In the beginning was the Word, and the Word was with God, and the Word was God...And the Word was made flesh, and dwelt among us" (John 1:1,14).

The Bible is a book that can literally heal you as you read it. The word of God actually does something to your physical body as you read it, believe it, and act on it.

Secondly, I believe in miracles because I have seen them all of my life. I was raised in the home of a spirit-filled pastor where prayer and fasting for miracles was the norm. The God of miracles began to demonstrate himself to my family through the prayer life and ministry of my grandfather, John Christopher Hagee. My father, Bythel Hagee, continued the practice of praying and fasting for miracles in his pastoral ministry, which spanned five decades. His church was built around the preaching of the Word and the mighty miracles of God that were manifested in the lives of his church members. His prayer partner was my mother, and when these two anointed prayer warriors began to come against disease and sickness, miracles happened.

I have also seen miracles in my own life and ministry, and that is what this book is all about.

The day came in my life when the phone rang and everything changed. The voice on the other end of the line was my mother, who said, "The doctor says I have cancer and I'm going to die."

The tumor was the size of a grapefruit and located in her colon. The prognosis was dreadful. She would need major surgery which would include a colostomy, spend several weeks in the hospital, and would have maybe twelve more months of marginal life before the cancer killed her.

Let me say here that I believe in doctors. They are wonderful people who have dedicated their lives to help suffering humanity. But doctors are not God; they are highly trained people who think only in terms of medical science. Medical science and faith healing operate in two completely different dimensions.

As advanced as medical technology has become, there are still limits to what doctors can do. Man's extremity is God's opportunity, however. When medical science comes to the end of its ability, we have the opportunity, as believers, to step into the supernatural realm and claim the benefits of our God.

These benefits include divine healing. King David wrote in Psalm 103, "Bless the Lord, O my soul, and forget not all his benefits: who forgiveth all thine iniquities; who healeth all thy diseases."

Have you ever interviewed job applicants? One of the first things they want to know is what benefits the employer offers. They want to know if the benefits include sick leave and paid vacation, health insurance and a retirement plan. When you make Jesus Christ Lord of your life, you sign on with an eternal employer who offers the greatest "benefits package" ever designed. His benefits include forgiveness for all your sins and healing for every disease (verse 3). He will redeem your life from destruction (verse 4) and renew your strength and youth (verse 5). The benefits just don't get any better!

When we received the news that my mother had cancer, we did what our family has been doing for generations: we gathered around her bed and started to pray. We began to curse that cancer in the name of Jesus of Nazareth. We declared that we would choose life and not death. We fasted and prayed daily.

Mother would walk the floor of her home reading out loud the sacred scriptures that promised her healing. This is important to do, because the healing power of God is released in your body when you hear, read or pray the scriptures aloud.

The date for surgery arrived. We all gathered around Mother's bed for one last prayer. We felt enough victory in that room to snatch the gates of hell off at the hinges!

The surgeon said the operation would last at least four hours, and that she might not survive the surgery. When your doctor tells you the worst, your first enemy to fight will be fear. Speak aloud these scriptures: "For God hath not given us the spirit of fear; but of power, and of love, and of a sound mind" (2 Timothy 1:7); and "Fear thou not; for I am with thee: be not dismayed; for I am thy God: I will strengthen thee; yea, I will help thee; yea, I will uphold thee with the right hand of my righteousness" (Isaiah 41:10).

Mother was wheeled into surgery and we went to the waiting room. The doctor came out after only an hour and a half. Instantly, we knew the news was either going to be very good, or very bad. The doctor smiled and said, "The tumor had shrunk to the size of a walnut. We removed it successfully, and we didn't have to do a colostomy."

Instead of several weeks in the hospital, Mother only stayed three days. Within two weeks she was back at her job in the public schools. Eight years after her surgery she is still cancer-free, healed by the mighty power of a miracle-working God.

Do I believe in miracles? Yes, and I know beyond any shadow of a doubt that miracles are for us today.

Miracles are for today

Perhaps you have come from a church background where the pastor taught that the age of miracles has passed. That falsehood has been pounded into the minds of millions of evangelical Christians—but it has absolutely no basis of truth in scripture. From the time of Jesus Christ miracles have happened, are happening, and will continue to happen until our Lord returns and miracles are no longer needed.

Malachi wrote, "I am the Lord, I change not" (3:6). Hebrews 13:8 says that Jesus Christ is "the same yesterday, and today, and for ever." What Jesus did by the Sea of Galilee, he can still do today. There is not one verse in the Bible that implies that "the day of miracles has passed." Exactly the opposite is true.

If miracles were supposed to cease with the apostles, why did James, under the direction of the Holy Spirit, command the church to pray for the sick? "Is any sick among you? let him call for the elders of the church; and let them pray over him, anointing him with oil in the name of the Lord: and the prayer of faith shall save the sick, and the Lord shall raise him up" (James 5:14-15). James didn't say, "Now you can only do this until such and such a date, and then it won't work any more because the age of miracles will have passed."

The apostles fully anticipated that miracles would continue forever by the laying on of hands and anointing with oil in the name of the Lord Jesus. James declared that the prayer of faith would be confirmed with miracles. There is no expiration date on the "prayer of faith coupon." It doesn't say, "Offer good while supplies last," or "Void after 12-31-91. Only one coupon per customer per visit."

Notice that James asked if there were any "sick among you." He was talking to believers. He knew that believers would be attacked by sickness, but that their first line of defense is to believe God for healing. We are not to call every doctor in town and then try God after everything else has failed. God is to be our first choice, not our last chance.

Jesus said, "Verily, verily, I say unto you, He that believeth on me, the works that I do shall he do also; and *greater works* than these shall he do; because I go unto my Father" (John 14:12). Jesus, who raised the dead and

healed the sick, said that those who believe on him would
do even *greater works* than he did. Do you believe on the
Lord? Then you have Jesus' promise that you will do
greater works. You won't do these greater works if you
don't believe what he said, but his miracle-working power
is available to you if you will receive it in faith. "Nothing
shall be impossible" to those who believe (Matt. 17:20).

Mark 16:17-18 states, "And these signs shall follow
them that believe; In my name shall they cast out devils;
they shall speak with new tongues; They shall take up
serpents; and if they drink any deadly thing, it shall not
hurt them; they *shall* lay hands on the sick, and they *shall*
recover."

The message is crystal clear. Miracles are for today, for
every believer.

Doubt and unbelief are viruses that will kill every
miracle in the birth canal. If you need a miracle, you must
conquer doubt and unbelief and release your faith. Don't
be deceived by the lie that it takes tremendous faith to
receive a miracle and that you could never have that much
faith. Every believer has been given faith to some degree
(Rom. 12:3) and your tiny, mustard-seed faith is big
enough to move mountains and pull up trees by their roots
(Matt. 17:20, Luke 17:6).

When your faith seems small, remember that the God in
whom your faith rests is bigger than you can ever imagine.
Don't put your faith in your faith, put your faith in God.
Your ability to believe is not the issue, God's ability to work
miracles is. Your ability to believe cannot outstrip God's
ability to perform.

In other words, you can't believe for something that is so
big that God cannot do it. "With men it is impossible, but
not with God; for with God *all things are possible*" (Mark
10:27). That is the God in whom you have faith, and if you
will release your faith, you will receive a miracle.

Extremes in the healing message

Extremists have hurt the healing message and caused many to turn away from it. People run around preaching two or three verses while ignoring the rest of God's word. Any fool can take a verse out of context and make a spiritual platform out of it.

For example, you can prove from scripture that David rode a motorcycle: Psalm 108:9 says "over Philistia will I Triumph." You can prove the apostles drove a Honda: Acts 2:1 says they were all in one Accord. And you can prove that suicide is God's will for your life: Matthew 27:5 says that Judas hanged himself and Luke 10:37 says, "Go and do thou likewise." You may think these examples are silly, and they are, but entire denominations have been built on a single Bible verse taken out of context.

One extreme in the healing message is that God heals everyone all the time, and if you're not healed it must mean that you don't have enough faith or that you have sin in your life. The other extreme is that God never heals anyone, for any reason. Both of these extremes are flat out wrong. Let's look at what the Bible says.

The fifth chapter of John's gospel tells of Jesus' visit to the pool of Bethesda. The pool was surrounded with sick people waiting for the waters to be troubled. Jesus healed only one man and left the others there sick. Why? Because God has a sovereign will.

Elijah lived during the greatest depression in Old Testament times. There were many, many widows who were starving, but God sent his prophet and his provision to only one. Why? Because God has a sovereign will.

There were many, many lepers during the time of Elisha, but only one was healed. Why? Because God has a sovereign will.

Paul, who had a rather successful New Testament ministry, prayed for his co-worker Trophimus. Paul was a man of faith who worked many miracles through God's power, but 2 Timothy 4:20 says Trophimus was still sick after Paul prayed for him, and Paul had to leave him behind in Miletus. Why? Did Paul not have enough faith? Did he not pray according to the right formula? Listen, you can name it and claim it, you can blab it and grab it, you can dance and prance until you get blisters on your feet—but you will not force God to function by your faith formula. God will do what he wants to do, when he wants to do it, and you can't kick him in the shins and have your way. God has a sovereign will. To say that God heals everyone all the time, and you must have sin in your life if your prayer isn't answered, is simply not scriptural.

Neither is the other extreme, that God never heals anyone. Sixty times in the Old Testament God introduces himself as healer. In his first sermon, Jesus Christ introduced himself as healer. If Hebrews 13:8 is true, if Jesus Christ really is "the same yesterday, and today, and for ever," then he is still healer and healing is still available for you and me.

The nature of miracles

Miracles are not the by-product of emotion, and miracles do not happen just because you need one. Miracles are the by-product of meeting God's conditions. Many people feel in a time of crisis that if they wring their hands enough, or beg God intently enough, or crawl down the steps to some shrine, God will hear their prayer. That's wrong. God does not respond to your emotional intensity, and he does not respond because your need is urgent. God responds when you meet his spiritual conditions for miracles to happen.

Let me explain what I mean in the physical dimension, and then I'll explain it in the spiritual dimension.

If I fill a tray with water and place it in the freezer compartment of my refrigerator, what will happen? The water will become ice. Is that a miracle? No, it's the only thing the physical laws of nature will let happen. When the water in the tray reaches a temperature of 32°, it has met the physical conditions for freezing. The water changes from liquid to solid, and remains in that frozen state as long as the physical conditions of temperature are maintained.

Just as there are physical laws in the natural realm, there are spiritual laws in the supernatural realm. Physical laws govern how things work in the natural, and spiritual laws govern how things work in the supernatural. Physical laws, however, are subject to spiritual laws, and a miracle occurs when supernatural forces are brought to bear on the natural realm.

We all know something about the physical laws of mathematics. I learned the principles of addition and subtraction in the first grade, just like you did. Two plus two equals four. Every time. That's the law of addition. And four minus two equals two. Every time. That's the law of subtraction. But the physical laws of addition and subtraction are subject to supernatural laws. Let me give you an example from the Bible.

All four gospels record the miracle of the loaves and fishes. Jesus was in the countryside teaching a large crowd of over 5,000 people. It was getting late in the day, and the disciples came to him and said, "Master, we should send these people away so they can go into the villages to get something to eat." Jesus replied, "Why don't you feed them instead?"

The disciples couldn't figure out what to do—they certainly didn't have enough money to buy food for that many people, and the only food they could lay their hands on was five loaves of bread and two fishes. But they took what they had to Jesus. After he told the large crowd to sit down on the grass, Jesus blessed the loaves and fishes and told the disciples to distribute the food to the crowd.

Now it could be that when Jesus said "Amen," loaves and fishes started popping up everywhere until there was a huge pile of food big enough to feed 5,000 people. But one of God's conditions for receiving a miracle (we'll cover these in the next chapter) is that you must act on your faith. I think what happened was more along these lines: when Jesus blessed the five loaves and two fishes, he handed the same five loaves and two fishes back to the disciples and said, "Now go feed the crowd." And when the disciples started walking into the crowd, they were holding one basket with five loaves of bread, and one basket with two fishes.

The first man to be fed took one of the five loaves, and when the disciples looked down there were six loaves left in the basket. Another man took one of the two fishes, and when the disciples looked down there were four fishes left in the basket. They handed out another loaf and there were eight loaves left. Another fish was handed out and there were six fishes left. After several people had been fed and the food kept multiplying, Peter looked at John and said, "I think you'd better go find some more baskets, because we're going to have leftovers when this is done."

Now I don't mean to be disrespectful to scripture by putting words in the disciples' mouths. I'm just trying to imagine how Jesus multiplied five loaves of bread and two fishes into enough food to feed 5,000 people. While I can't tell you exactly how it happened, I do know this: when Jesus prayed and the disciples acted in faith, God's supernatural law of multiplication smashed the natural law of subtraction to smithereens. Now that's my kind of "new math."

The same thing happens in miracles of healing. Sickness and disease operate according to physical laws, but the physical laws of sickness and disease are subject to spiritual laws of divine healing.

For example, cancer cells multiply and spread throughout the body because that's how they work in the physical dimension. When the cancer spreads until it destroys all your healthy cells and can no longer be removed from your body by medical procedures, then you will die. That's how cancer works in our bodies, because cancer operates according to physical laws.

As I have said, my mother was diagnosed with a tumor

the size of a grapefruit. We cursed that tumor in Jesus' name and prayed for a miracle. The physical law of multiplication of cancerous cells was broken as the power of God started dividing those cancer cells. By the time of her surgery, the tumor had shrunk to the size of a walnut. Why? Because physical laws are subject to spiritual laws and miracles happen when you meet God's conditions.

Chapter 2

Meeting God's Conditions For A Miracle

As we have seen, supernatural laws will override natural laws when spiritual conditions are met. When you meet God's spiritual conditions for miracles, then miracles have to happen, because God operates by spiritual laws in the supernatural realm.

That makes it extremely important to learn what the word of God says about the conditions for receiving a miracle, doesn't it? I believe there are eight spiritual conditions that must be met for God's supernatural laws to intervene in the natural realm.

Condition #1: Accept and obey the word of God

Your healing begins with the absolute acceptance of and obedience to the word of God. Let's examine the scriptural evidence to support this statement.

Proverbs 4:22 says, "[My words] are life unto those that find them, and health to all their flesh." God's word is the source of spiritual and physical life. "Flesh" refers to your physical body, and God says here that he will bring health to your physical body through his word.

"My son, forget not my law [my word]; but let thine heart

keep my commandments: for length of days, and long life, and peace, shall they add to thee...It [my word] shall be health to thy navel, and marrow to thy bones" (Proverbs 3:1-2 and 8).

Why does God say that his word is health to your navel? The navel is where the umbilical cord attaches an unborn child to its mother. The navel is the source of nutrition while a baby is in its mother's womb. You have a spiritual navel, so to speak, that attaches you to God and is your source of spiritual nourishment. The spiritual food you eat will sustain your spiritual life, as physical food sustains your physical life. More than that, when you eat the spiritual food of God's word, it will bring you physical health as well as spiritual health.

When an apple is pulled from a tree, it stops receiving the nutrition of the tree. The apple is good to eat for a while, but it eventually begins to decompose and rot. When you pull yourself away from the word of God, which is your spiritual nutrition, you begin to decompose spiritually. When you stay away from the word of God long enough, you get to a place where you don't believe in miracles and where you are so spiritually insensitive that you can't feel God or hear God. If you are spiritually comatose, you can never receive a miracle from God, because you cannot meet God's conditions.

Psalm 119:92-93 says, "Unless thy law [thy word] had been my delights, I should then have perished in mine affliction. I will never forget thy precepts [thy words]: for with them thou hast quickened me [preserved my life]." Psalm 107:20– "He sent his word and healed them." Psalm 43:5– "Why art thou cast down, O my soul? And why art thou disquieted within me? Hope in God: for I shall yet praise him, who is the health of my countenance, and my God." Jeremiah 30:17– "I will restore health unto thee, and I will heal thee of thy wounds."

Isaiah 40:31 says, "They that wait upon the Lord shall renew their strength." The Hebrew word for *strength* means *life force*. If you want your life force, your energy factor, to be renewed every day, wait upon the Lord. That life force is the source of your physical, as well as your spiritual, strength.

There are many reports of healings in the Bible that demonstrate the absolute power of God's word over disease. Some of these biblical reports are not easily understood by gentile believers, who do not have the cultural and spiritual background to understand them. Let's look at some examples.

Matthew 8:35-36 says, "And when the men of that place had knowledge of him, they sent out into all that country round about, and brought unto him all that were diseased; And besought him that they might only *touch the hem of his garment:* and as many as touched were made perfectly whole." Luke 6:19 says, "And the whole multitude *sought to touch him:* for there went virtue out of him, and healed them all." Matthew 9, Mark 5 and Luke 8 all record the story of the woman with "an issue of blood" who *touched the border of his garment* (Luke 8:43) and was instantly healed.

Why did these sick people want to touch Jesus? What were they reaching for when they touched the hem or the border of his garment? The key to these scriptures is found in the Greek word *kraspedon*, which can be translated hem, or border, or edge of a garment. It is this Greek word which was always used in the Septuagint (the Greek translation which was in use during the time of Christ and the early Christian era) to translate the Hebrew word *tzitzit*, which refers to the ritual tassels worn on the clothing of all Jewish males age thirteen and older.

The wearing of the *tzitzit* was commanded by God in Numbers 15:37-40. It is observed to this day by devout Jews. The prayer shawl is an outer garment with the ritual fringes and *tzitzit*, which are the tassels on the four corners, that represent the 613 commandments of the Torah that righteous Jews obey. The prayer shawl is worn as a reminder of God's word and God's will.

In Hebrew geometria, every letter of the alphabet has a numerical significance. This is scripturally verified by

John the Revelator, who wrote that the coming antichrist could be identified by calculating the numerology of his name. "If anyone has insight, let him calculate the number of the beast, for it is a man's number. His number is 666." (Rev. 13:18)

The *tzitzit* are made up of a series of knots and coils in such a way that they "spell out" the name *Jehovah God,* and every Jewish person knows how to read the message hidden in the *tzitzit* on a prayer shawl.

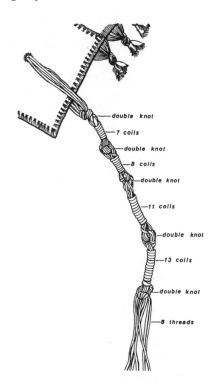

double knot

7 coils

double knot

8 coils

double knot

11 coils

double knot

13 coils

double knot

8 threads

Artist's rendering of the *tzitzit* on a prayer shawl

Jesus was a rabbi and he wore the prayer shawl every day of his life. When sick people reached out to "touch the hem of his garment," they were reaching for the tassels on his prayer shawl. They were reaching for something that represented the word of God. They knew that the word of God was "life...and health to all their flesh" (Prov. 4:22).

They knew that the commandments of God were "health to their navel and marrow to their bones" (Prov. 3:8).

These sick people knew that if they could touch the word of God, they would be healed. And they were. Everyone who touched Jesus' prayer shawl was healed. And as they reached for the representation of the word of God by touching the *tzitzit* on Jesus' prayer shawl, they actually touched the Word of God Himself, because Jesus was the very word of God made flesh to dwell among us (John 1:14).

Condition #2: Believe that it is God's will to heal you

Millions of sick people are being robbed of their miracle of healing by praying, "Lord, if it's your will, heal me." Why don't we let the word of God settle this issue.

The gospel of Matthew records that a man with leprosy came to Jesus and said, "Lord, if you will, you can make me clean." Jesus reached out and touched the man, and said, "I will. Be clean!" (Matthew 8:2-3). Jesus confirms in this scripture that he was and is willing to heal.

Actually, God indicated his willingness to heal long before Jesus began his healing ministry on earth. The earliest promise of healing is found in Exodus 15:26, "If thou wilt diligently hearken to the voice of the Lord thy God [remember the importance of the word of God in healing?], and wilt do that which is right in his sight, and wilt give ear to his commandments, and keep all his statutes, I will put none of these diseases upon thee, which I have brought upon the Egyptians: for I am the Lord that healeth thee."

Where and when was this promise made? It was made to the children of Israel as they left Egypt and started on their journey to the promised land. This promise is parallel to Christ's healing of disease at the beginning of his ministry. The promise to the children of Israel came immediately after they passed through the Red Sea, which is a type or foreshadowing of water baptism for the believer. God is saying to every believer, "The very first thing I offer you upon redemption is divine healing from all diseases."

Writing about the events of the Old Testament, Paul said, "Now all these things happened unto them for examples; and they are written for our admonition [instruction]" (1 Cor. 10:11). What does that mean? That the same miracles God gave to the children of Israel are intended for every believer. Sickness belongs to the "Egyptians," not to the children of God. If we return spiritually to Egypt, we return to its perils, including sickness and disease.

Get it fixed in your mind that God wants to heal you. Don't allow your thoughts to dwell on your sickness. Allow your thoughts to dwell on the word of God. 3 John 2 says, "Beloved, I wish above all things that you may prosper and be in health, even as your soul prospers." I want you to understand that health is the law of the kingdom of God. God said he is *Jehovah Rophe,* the Lord our Healer, and he sent Jesus Christ to be our Great Physician. Whatever is wrong with you—heart, soul, mind or body—he *can* heal you, he *will* heal you, and he wants to heal you today.

Condition #3: Believe that your healing has been paid for at the cross

The cross of Christ is the centerpiece for the gospel. Every blessing that we enjoy as believers comes directly from what Jesus accomplished at the cross.

He took our guilt that we might be forgiven. He took our poverty that we might be rich toward God. He took our rejection that we might be accepted as sons and daughters of the living God. He took our sickness and disease that we might have divine health.

Isaiah's prophecy of the messiah in chapter 53 was fulfilled at the cross of Christ. Verse 5 declares that "with his stripes we are healed." That is a present tense verb: we are healed. We are being healed right now by the stripes that Jesus took on his back nearly 2,000 years ago.

Verse 4 says that he bore our griefs and carried our sorrows (King James version). A literal translation of the Hebrew in this verse is that Jesus carried our sickness and disease off to another location. Read the whole chapter of Isaiah 53 and then read Leviticus 16. It will become clear that Isaiah is saying that the messiah is our scapegoat, the animal that symbolically carried away the sins of the Hebrews on the Day of Atonement. Not only has the messiah carried away our sins, Isaiah says, he carried away our sickness and disease as well.

Now how do I know that Isaiah really meant that we have been saved from *physical* sickness and disease and not just *spiritual* sickness? Because I can read! It plainly says in the eighth chapter of Matthew that Jesus healed the sick because Isaiah said that's what the messiah would do. In chapter 8, Matthew recounts three specific healings of Jesus: a leper, the centurion's servant, and Peter's mother-in-law. Then he goes on to say, "They brought unto him many that were possessed with devils: and he cast out the spirits with his word, *and healed all that were sick: That it might be fulfilled which was spoken by Isaiah the prophet,* saying, Himself took our infirmities, and bare our sicknesses" (v. 16-17).

How could God make it any plainer than that? If you have believed that Jesus died on the cross to purchase your salvation only, and not your healing, you have believed a lie. In the same way that you got saved, by faith in Jesus Christ, you can get healed. He purchased your healing with great pain and suffering, with his very blood—why would you not believe that he wants you to be healed?

Condition #4: Act on your faith

Once you have accepted that the word of God demonstrates that it is God's will to heal you and that Jesus has paid for your healing on the cross, you must then act on your faith.

Faith is the currency of heaven. Going to God without faith is like going to Sears without money—you can look around, but you can't buy anything. If you don't activate your faith, you can watch everybody around you receive a miracle while you stay sick.

Hebrews 11:6 says that "without faith it is impossible to please him: for he that cometh to God must believe that he is, and that he is a rewarder of them that diligently seek him." James 2:17 says that if you don't put your faith to work, your faith is dead.

Everything God has for you comes at the cost of faith. Faith is the daring of the soul to go farther than your physical eyes can see. Faith is the daring of the soul to go farther than your carnal mind can comprehend. Did you know that when the first automobile was manufactured there were scientists who believed that if you went faster than 35 miles an hour your body would explode? That sounds strange today, but that's what they believed. It took somebody with enough daring to go beyond what everybody could see or understand to invent the automobile. Now you can go 35 miles an hour in reverse—at least my car will.

All of us have a limit to our faith. But there is no limitation to what God can do when we release our faith. So if you need a miracle, you have to first believe that God still works miracles and that he wants you to have one. Then you have to ask God in faith for a miracle, and then you have to act on your faith.

When Jesus healed the man with a withered hand, he first told him, "Stretch forth your hand." The man did, and the withered hand was restored (Matt. 12:13). Jesus commanded the man to act on his faith by stretching forth his hand. By obeying Jesus, the man was showing that he had faith that Jesus could and would heal him.

When Jesus healed the paralytic, he told him, "Arise, take up your bed, and go to your house." And the man did just that (Matthew 9:2-8). He acted in faith and he was healed.

In Luke 17, ten lepers asked Jesus to have mercy on them. He said, "Go show yourselves unto the priests." He did not lay hands on them. He did not pray for them. He did not tell them they were healed. He just told them to go see the priest, which is what the law required after you had been cured of a disease. Verse 14 says that *"as they went, they were cleansed."*

The apostles followed the pattern of Jesus. Peter and John told the lame man at the temple gate, "In the name of Jesus Christ of Nazareth, rise up and walk." When Peter took the lame man by his right hand and lifted him up, his bones "received strength" and he went into the temple with them, "walking, and leaping, and praising God" (Acts 3:6-8).

In Lystra, there was a man who was lame from birth. He had never walked. He listened raptly as Paul preached the word of God. Recognizing that the crippled man had faith to be healed, Paul stopped preaching and shouted, "Stand upright on your feet!" This man, who had never walked before in his life, jumped up and started walking (Acts 14:8-10). But understand this. If he had not acted on his faith, he would have sat there crippled the rest of his life.

When you are believing God for a miracle, you need to focus on faith and not on feelings. You need to focus on the biblical report and not your medical report. Believe what the word of God says about healing. Quote it out loud, and say it over and over. "Faith cometh by hearing, and hearing by the word of God" (Rom. 10:17). If you want to increase your faith, increase the time you spend in God's word. As you begin to release your faith, you will feel the supernatural, life-giving power of the Holy Spirit invade your life, your mind and your body. You will begin to be well from that moment.

When the Holy Spirit whispers in your ear to "take up your bed and walk," do it! Act on your faith. The devil won't tell you to get up off your sick bed—he wants to keep you down. But when you start releasing your faith, the Spirit will prompt you to take action.

The first step of faith you take may be very small. You may be so sick that all you can do is sit up in your hospital bed and hang your feet off the side. Do it, in faith, and before long you'll be holding on to somebody and walking around your room, and after that you'll be walking down the hospital corridor, and one day you'll walk out of that hospital. You don't have to throw your crutches out the window or flush your medication down the toilet to exercise your faith. You may receive your healing instantly (that's called a miracle), or you may receive it gradually (that's a gift of healing). What difference does it make as long as you get well? Let the Holy Spirit be your partner in faith and lead you every step of the way to your miracle.

Condition #5: Confess your sins

Remember when we talked about the benefits of God? We looked at Psalm 103, which says, "Bless the Lord, O my soul, and forget not all his benefits: who forgiveth all thine iniquities; who healeth all thy diseases" (verses 2-3). Healing is the second benefit. The first benefit is forgiveness for sin. There is a relationship between your spiritual man and your physical man. That's why many of the scriptures on healing are tied in with salvation.

3 John 2 says, "Beloved, I wish above all things that you prosper, and be in health, even as thy soul prospers." God wants us to be healthy, but he puts a tag on it that says, "even as your soul prospers."

We've already looked at some of the extremes in the healing message, one of which is that God always heals, and if you're not healed it must be because there's sin in your life. Let me state again that not all sickness is the result of sin, and just because you haven't been healed yet does not mean there is sin in your life. But unconfessed sin can stop you from receiving a miracle.

Any time we're praying, especially when we're praying for God's miracle-working power to be manifested in our lives, we need to examine our hearts for hidden sins. We need to receive the benefit of forgiveness before we receive the benefit of healing.

Isaiah said, "Look, God does not need a hearing aid." (That's the Hagee translation.) "But," he said, "your iniquities have separated between you and your God, and your sins have hid his face from you, that he will not hear" (Isa. 59:1).

When we have confessed our sins, we can pray with confidence that God hears us and will answer us. "Beloved, if our heart condemn us not, then have we confidence toward God. And whatsoever we ask, we receive of him, because we keep his commandments, and do those things that are pleasing in his sight" (1 John 3:21-22).

When James instructed us to anoint with oil and pray for the sick, he also tied it in with confession of sin. "And the prayer of faith shall save the sick, and the Lord shall raise him up; and if he have committed sins, they shall be forgiven him. Confess your faults one to another, and pray one for another, that ye may be healed" (James 5:15-16).

Why is confession of sin so important to your healing? Because sin kills. "For the wages of sin is death" (Rom. 6:23). That verse is primarily talking about spiritual death and eternal separation from God. But it also implies physical death. The wages of alcohol and drug abuse is death by overdose or liver disease. The wages of tobacco is emphysema and lung cancer. The wages of promiscuity, homosexual or heterosexual, is death by AIDS or another sexually transmitted disease. We are living in an age where it is easy to see that sin kills.

Paul writes in Romans 8:13, "For if you live according to the sinful nature, you will die; but if by the Spirit you put to death the misdeeds of the body, you will live." The bottom line is this: sin kills; but forgiveness of sin brings life.

Miracle killers are stalking your life: resentment, bitterness, unforgiveness, lying, tale bearing, murmuring, rebellion against spiritual authority, being an accuser of the brethren, having a critical spirit, and all manner of sins. But you can wipe out these miracle killers with one prayer for forgiveness. Don't let unconfessed sin keep you from receiving your miracle from God.

Condition #6: Denounce the kingdom of darkness

Thirty years ago Americans didn't believe there was a real devil. Today they're worshipping him from coast to coast.

There is a very real devil, and his objective is to steal, kill and destroy (John 10:10). That's why almost every healing service Jesus held began with deliverance from evil spirits. Matthew 8:16 says, "When evening came, many who were demon possessed were brought to him and he drove out the spirits with a word and healed all the sick." The Bible says that "many" were demonized and had to be delivered before healing was possible.

When you read the gospels, you discover that about one-fourth of Jesus' ministry was dedicated to the control of evil spirits. He was dealing with normal, Jewish people who went to synagogue on the Sabbath, tithed up to 30% of their income, and were law-abiding and clean-living. But he recognized the power of Satan to control areas of their lives.

You cannot have the benefits of God and dabble in the occult, or any form of mind control, ESP, Ouija boards, Tarot cards, or horoscopes, not to mention witchcraft and satanism. If you have participated in any of these things, you need deliverance before healing is possible.

Condition #7: Reject intellectual idolatry

We have become a skeptical and doubt-infected society through intellectual idolatry. Intellectual idolatry is the worship of your opinions or philosophies over the truth of the word of God. 1 Samuel 15:23 says that "stubbornness is as idolatry." Who is stubborn? The person who will not change his opinion even when he hears the truth of God's word.

The intellectual idolator is one who has made his thoughts, his opinions and his philosophies his gods. He chooses doubt over faith. He chooses death over life. He chooses science over the supernatural. The day will come when he needs a miracle, and his intellectualism will be revealed for what it truly is: idolatry.

You may value your opinions highly, but they do not affect reality! Fire burns, whether you believe it or not. Sin kills, whether you believe it or not. Miracles happen, whether you believe it or not. And God heals, whether you believe it or not. If you don't believe God heals, it's a certainty you won't be on the receiving end of a miracle. You need to quit trusting in your ideas and opinions and start trusting in God.

> *Trust in the Lord with all your heart*
> *   and lean not on your own understanding;*
> *in all your ways acknowledge him,*
> *   and he will make your paths straight.*
> *Do not be wise in your own eyes:*
> *   fear the Lord and shun evil.*
> *This will bring health to your body*
> *   and nourishment to your bones.*
>   Proverbs 3:5-8

The death of King Asa illustrates the danger of intellectual idolatry. Asa started his reign on the right note, by tearing down the pagan idols and altars. He urged Judah to repent from idolatry and the Lord blessed his reign with peace and prosperity (2 Chron. 14:2-7). When the Ethiopian armies came against him, Asa sought the Lord, who brought a great victory (14:11-12). Asa repaired the altar of the Lord (15:8) and he even removed his grandmother from her position as queen mother, because she worshipped idols (15:16).

For thirty-five years there was peace in Asa's kingdom. But some time during those thirty-five years Asa got to thinking too highly of his own opinions. He became a victim of his intellectual idolatry. In the thirty-sixth year of his reign, the king of Israel came against Asa. Instead of seeking the Lord this time, Asa bought a treaty with the king of Syria and paid for it with silver and gold out of the temple treasuries. When the prophet of the Lord rebuked him, Asa threw the prophet in prison.

Three years later, when Asa needed a miracle, he had philosophies but no faith. Here's the end of his story, straight from the word of God: "In the thirty-ninth year of his reign Asa was afflicted with a disease in his feet. Though his disease was severe, even in his illness he did not seek help from the Lord, but only from the physicians. Then in the forty-first year of his reign Asa died." (16:12-13)

Asa took his fashionable philosophies to the grave with him, when a little old-fashioned faith would have brought him a miracle.

Condition #8: Recognize the role of the Holy Spirit in healing

Few people understand the role of the Holy Spirit in the healing process. We think of Jesus as our healer, which he is. Jesus paid the price for our healing at the cross, but we receive his healing power through the operation of the Holy Spirit.

"And if the spirit of him who raised Jesus from the dead is living in you, he who raised Christ from the dead will also give life to your mortal bodies through his Spirit, who lives in you" (Romans 8:11). It is the Holy Spirit who raised Jesus from the dead. That same Holy Spirit dwells in us, and will bring us the healing power of Jesus, as we receive it.

Many people are not healed because they reject the Holy Spirit in their lives and in their churches. Where the Holy Spirit is rejected, there will be no healing. One reason we have seen so many healings in our services at Cornerstone Church is that we invite the presence of the Holy Spirit to be manifested in our congregation. In the atmosphere of praise and worship, God the Holy Spirit descends like a gentle dove and begins to heal all who have released their faith and expect the power of God to come upon them.

Healing is one of the manifestations of the gifts of the spirit listed in the 12th chapter of 1 Corinthians. Nine gifts of the spirit are listed in this passage. These gifts fall into three major areas, and each of these areas has three specific gifts under it.

First, there are the speaking gifts: tongues, interpretation and prophecy. Next there are the doing gifts: faith, miracles and healing. Finally, there are the thinking gifts: wisdom, knowledge and discernment. This is the progression of the gifts of the Holy Spirit in your life. The speaking gifts require the least amount of supernatural faith, so they are usually the entry-level gifts. But as the Holy Spirit controls your speaking, he then begins to manifest himself in your doing, and then in your thinking.

This same progression is found historically in the church. It was around the turn of the century that the Holy Spirit began to be poured out in America. At a prayer meeting in Topeka, Kansas, on January 1, 1901, people seeking the Lord suddenly began to speak in other tongues as the Holy Spirit gave them utterance. The revival started to spread across the country, and a three-year revival meeting at the Azusa Street Mission in Los Angeles, California, launched the modern pentecostal movement. The speaking gifts of the spirit had been restored to the church in America.

Then about 1948 came the restoration of the doing gifts of faith, healing and miracles. Several major healing ministries began in America about this time, including Oral Roberts's ministry. He went to visit a tent meeting where one of his friends was preaching. The tent would hold 1,000 people, and for a pentecostal, that was a massive tent. His friend got sick and could not preach, so they asked Brother Oral to speak. He was pastoring a small church of fewer than 200 people at the time.

As he spoke, the Lord directed him to pray for some children that had come. He didn't know the children had come from a school for the deaf. He went down and began to pray for these children and each one of them began to speak. He didn't think anything about it, because he didn't know they were all deaf.

Someone from the press was there (they always are, God love them), so the tent meeting where the deaf children were healed was on the front page of the newspaper. The next night, that tent was full. And Oral Roberts just continued praying for the sick, and with signs and wonders, God supernaturally manifested a healing power through him.

The gift of healing God gave that man was one of the most real, genuine gifts I have ever seen. The healing ministries that began in 1948 marked the restoration of the doing gifts to the church in America.

Then in 1967 there was the outbreak of the thinking gifts of wisdom, knowledge and discernment. That is where the church happens to be at this point in time, because that is what is needed in our world. Satan has raised up his hosts in ESP, mind control, metaphysics and the occult. But God has restored the manifestations of the Holy Spirit so that we can know the unknowable. So the thinking gifts, which can play an important role in healing and deliverance, have also been restored to the church in these last days.

I believe we are entering into a time of great revival— the last great revival before the Lord returns. This revival is being accompanied by an outpouring of mighty miracles, and God's word is being confirmed with signs and wonders. Other pastors and church leaders are sensing the same thing: the church is being stirred up by the Holy Spirit and prepared for the return of our High Priest and King.

Everything that can be shaken will be shaken, and many will fall away, because this revival will also be accompanied by a great apostasy.

But what an exciting time to be alive! There's a miracle out there with your name on it. The Holy Spirit is "troubling the waters" and healing power is flowing. Get in that flow and receive your miracle...and then help someone else receive the miracle they need.

Chapter 3

Living in
Divine Health

Every time I visit someone in the hospital I thank God for health and healing. When I see people who are bedridden, I thank God for the ability to walk. When I see people on breathing machines, I thank God for the ability to breathe unassisted by medical devices. What a treasure it is to hold in my arms my healthy children. That is a blessing from God and I never take it for granted.

It is a pleasure to be able to get up every morning and go to work. Don't ever complain about having to get up in the morning. The time may come when you can't get out of bed, period. Thank God for the ability to get up and go to work and be an expression of God's health on earth.

A lot of people lose their health trying to gain wealth. Then they lose their wealth trying to regain health. You can avoid this trap if you will live by biblical principles. The Bible is the greatest health manual ever printed. You need to get it out from under your *TV Guide* and start reading it!

Let's look first at some of the reasons why health fails, and then what to do when your health fails.

Why health fails

Ignorance is one of the reasons our health fails. We continually push our bodies beyond its limits of endurance. Everything in life has a stress limit—why do we think our bodies are immune from the ill effects of too much stress? When you work a 90-hour week, live on junk food and don't get enough rest, your body will break down. A square meal is one based on the four food groups, not one that comes in a box from the drive-in window of the nearest fast food franchise. (By the way, the four food groups are not hamburgers, tacos, pizza and egg rolls.)

Arrogance is another reason health fails. When you know how to live healthy but don't, you are arrogantly defying the principles of God. Every time you put tobacco in your mouth you are inviting cancer to invade your body. With every puff of smoke you are threatening to kill yourself or those who are closest to you. Your diagnosis is already made; all that remains is to see whether it strikes your lungs, your mouth, your throat or a member of your family. In your dismay and despair you will have to face the fact that you chose death and disease, one puff or one chew at a time.

Two friends met who hadn't seen each other in a while. One of them, who was quite large, said to the other, who was very slim, "You look like you have been living in the land of famine." The skinny friend replied, "You look like you caused it all by yourself!" Being overweight comes from overeating. It is arrogant disobedience of God's principles of temperance and moderation. It brings on high blood pressure, heart disease, and a whole host of ailments. When you get sick, don't ask, "Why did God do this to me?" You asked for it one mouthful at a time, because you can dig your grave with your teeth.

The third reason health fails is sin. Spiritual health is the key to all health, mental, emotional and physical. You can't be at war with God, the architect of the human body, and be healthy. Not only will stress produce disease in your body, so will anger, hatred, bitterness and resentment. But the spiritual principles of love and forgiveness will produce a healthy mind and body.

There is another reason health fails: to demonstrate God's power. In the ninth chapter of John, Jesus healed a man who had been blind from birth. The disciples asked Jesus, "Who sinned, this man or his parents?" Jesus said neither one had sinned. The man was sick in order "that the works of God should be made manifest in him" (John 9:1-3).

Not all sickness and disease are caused by sin. Even the godly and those who "live right" get sick. God created Adam and Eve to live in divine health. But when Adam fell, physical death and disease, as well as spiritual death, entered the world.

Divine health is still God's plan for us. Jesus paid the price for our healing at the cross, and miracles of healing are given to us to demonstrate God's power. But it is a fact of life on this earth that good Christian men and women get sick and die before their time. It does not necessarily mean that they sinned or that they didn't have enough faith. It just means that they have received their ultimate healing in heaven, where there are no more tears and no more pain, no more sorrow or suffering.

Does that shake your faith? Do you think it's useless to pray for a miracle since God has a sovereign will and maybe you're going to be one of those who does not get healed? Is God playing some sort of spiritual roulette game with your life? It is not always our privilege to know why or how God does or does not do certain things in certain ways. God is not accountable to you or me. We do know that God and his word are unchangeable. We do know that he still works miracles and that it is his will to heal us—that is the plain truth of the word of God. We also know that "it is appointed unto man once to die" (Heb. 9:27).

God sovereignly determined my life span before I was born. Psalm 139:16 says, "All the days ordained for me were written in your book before one of them came to be." I do not know the number of days God has ordained for me. I am believing God for many years to work for him and enjoy life in good health. But I live each day ready to meet God. I pray on the authority of Psalm 91 that God will satisfy me with long life. But my life is not my own, it belongs to him. And because my life belongs to God, I refuse to let the devil steal even one of the days God has ordained for me. Every day I make the conscious decision to choose life, not death. With the Holy Spirit as my guide, I walk in obedience to the word of God. When I am sick, I ask the elders of my church to anoint me with oil and pray the prayer of faith. And when the last day that God ordains for me finally comes, I will draw my last breath praying and believing God for another miracle.

What to do when health fails

I overheard two people talking about their aches and pains. One of them told the other, "I'm doing so much better since I've changed doctors. This one is really good!" If you're sick, maybe you need to change doctors. Let me tell you about my divine doctor, the Great Physician—he's the Specialist of Specialists.

Without using a stethoscope he knows the condition of your heart. Without a brain scan he knows your every thought. Without blood tests he knows the chemistry of every cell in your body. He knows the number of hairs on your head, and he wants to be your divine doctor. "Come unto me, all ye that labor and are heavy laden, and I will give you rest" (Matt. 11:28).

The Great Physician makes house calls. "Call unto me, and I will answer thee, and show thee great and mighty things" (Jer. 33:3). You can call the Great Physician in the middle of the night and he will never say, "Take two aspirin and get some rest, then call me in the morning."

He is a doctor whose only fee is faith. "Without faith it is impossible to please him: for he that cometh to God must believe that he is, and that he is a rewarder of them that diligently seek him" (Heb. 11:6).

He is a doctor whose medical accomplishments have stunned the scientific community. Modern technology may allow man to produce a baby in a test tube, but my doctor created a man from a fist full of dirt—without the benefit of a research grant. My doctor heals the sick and raises the dead. He's never lost a case, and he wants to take care of you!

No matter how desperate your diagnosis, no matter how severe your symptoms, the Great Physician has a remedy for what ails you. He has written a manual on miraculous cures—have you read it lately? His prescription is prayer—have you taken your medicine today?

Chapter 4

The Healing Ministry of Jesus

If you're not living in divine health, if your health has failed and you need a miracle, I want to pray with you at the end of this chapter. First, however, I want to help build your faith by looking at the healing ministry of Jesus.

There are some popular misconceptions about healing that need to be debunked. A lot of people today have faith formulas. They think that God only works in a certain way. In their thinking, to be healed you have to pray the right words in the right order, or quote the right scriptures the right number of times, or go to the right faith healer or miracle rally. In their attempt to manufacture or manipulate faith, they limit God.

The good news is that God never has been, and never will be, limited by your attempts to figure him out. God heals in many ways, some of which may never have occurred to anybody yet, so you might as well trust God to rise to the occasion instead of trying to make him conform to your cookie cutter mold. You can't come up with a case that is too hard for the Great Physician. He can't be stumped. And his healing power cannot be limited by your attempts to formularize his methods.

How Jesus healed

Let's look first at *how* Jesus healed. In Matthew 8:16 Jesus healed en masse. He was talking to a massive congregation and when he pronounced a healing prayer, they began to get well all over the building. Then in Matthew 9 he healed them one at a time.

Sometimes Jesus laid hands on the sick, sometimes they touched him. Sometimes he healed with his word and not his hands. He even healed those who were not present at the time, like the centurion's servant. The centurion said to Jesus, "Lord, speak the word only, and my servant shall be healed" (Matt. 8:8). This man understood the authority of Jesus' word, and Jesus commended his faith.

What does that mean for you today? Simply that there is no distance in prayer. If you're in Texas and you have a son in California and a daughter in New York and both are sick, you can pray the prayer of faith, send it to the throne of grace, and the throne of grace will send it back to California and New York. They will be healed in Jesus' name because there is no distance in prayer.

Look at the different ways Jesus healed blindness. In Matthew 9:29 and 20:34 he touched the eyes of two blind men and they immediately received their sight. In Mark 10:52 and Luke 18:42 Jesus simply spoke to Bartimaeus and he immediately received his sight. In Mark 8:22-25 a blind man came to Jesus in Bethsaida to be healed. Jesus took him outside the town, spit on the man's eyes and laid hands on him. When Jesus asked the man if he could see anything, he replied that he could see people, but they looked like trees walking around. So Jesus touched his eyes again, and the second time he looked up he could see clearly.

In John 9, Jesus and the disciples were in Jerusalem and they passed by a man who had been born blind. Jesus spit on the ground and made mud out of the dirt and saliva. He put the mud on the man's eyes and told him to go wash in the pool of Siloam. The man did as Jesus commanded and his sight was restored.

This was not some off-the-wall method of healing, by the way. The Jews believed that the first-born son had healing virtue in his spittle. So when Jesus spit in the dirt and put that spittle on the blind man, he was testifying that he was the first-born son of his heavenly father. That's why he did it, and that's why the man was healed.

If Jesus were to do that today, a bunch of preachers would be lined up for question and answer time. "What's the ratio of spit and dirt?" "Do you put it on the left eye first, or the right eye first?" "Do you say anything special before or after you put the mud on?" Somebody would analyze it and put it in a formula and write a bestselling book called *Healing With Spit And Dirt: How To Receive Your Mud Miracle.*

Let me tell you something. God does not dance when you play the right tune. He has a thousand ways to answer every prayer you pray, so don't try to limit him with religious formulas. Release God to be God and let his supernatural power flow into your life.

What Jesus healed

Look at *what* Jesus healed. He healed every kind of sickness and disease. He not only gave sight to blind eyes, he caused deaf ears to hear and gave speech to the mute. The Bible record proves he is the healer of bones and muscles and nerves and every crippling disease. Withered hands were restored, paralyzed legs began to move and fused spinal columns were loosened. Those who were bent and stooped over were made straight at Jesus' touch. Those who couldn't get up on their own were raised up by his word.

Impossible medical cases were no match for Jesus. He cured the incurable, including a woman who had been hemorrhaging for 12 years. Mark said she had spent all her money on doctors, and instead of getting better she got worse. Luke, who was himself a doctor, diagnosed her as incurable. "No one could heal her," Dr. Luke said (8:43). No one except Jesus, that is.

Luke also records that Jesus healed ten lepers all at once (Luke 17). This mass healing impressed Dr. Luke. If Jesus had only healed one leper, the skeptics would have said it was a medical fluke, or a misdiagnosis. He healed all ten of them at once so there could be no scientific argument. They went to present themselves to the priest and there was no escaping the fact that God had done it, and done it instantly.

Jesus heals every sickness and disease, no matter what the cause. If it is caused by sin, Jesus heals it. If it is caused by an evil spirit, Jesus heals it. When the doctors don't know what caused the sickness, he can still heal it.

The Great Physician not only restores health, he recreates body parts. If your doctor says the reason your son can't hear is that he does not have a stapes, therefore it's impossible for him to ever hear, look right back at your doctor and say, "I serve a Great Physician who can create a stapes, and in Jesus' name I release him to do it. My son will hear in the name of the Son of God."

What about diseases that weren't even heard of in Bible days? What about cancer? What about multiple sclerosis? What about leukemia? What about AIDS? There is no such thing as an incurable disease with God. There is no virus that the healing power of Jesus cannot wipe out. There is no cancer cell that can spread faster than the healing power of Jesus can destroy it. Your immune system has not gotten so out of kilter that Jesus cannot fix it.

Our Great Physician took a handful of dirt and made you from scratch. He knows every blood cell in your body, every hair on your head is numbered. God knew about leukocytes and T-cells before doctors ever did. Hebrews 4:12 says his word can penetrate your joints and the very marrow of your bones. That's right, God was in the bone marrow transplant business long before doctors ever discovered how to do it. What we see as insurmountable doesn't even cause God to raise his eyebrows.

Jesus is the source of life

Jesus even healed the cases that the doctors lost, because he is the source of life itself. He said, "I have come that you may have life, and have it to the full" (John 10:10). "I am the resurrection, and the life" (John 11:25). He called Lazarus forth from the grave. Lazarus was dead and buried, but Jesus gave him back life. Jesus stopped a funeral procession one day. He raised a widow's son from death and changed that funeral procession into a parade of celebration. Ultimately, Jesus raised himself from the dead and presented himself as the story of life.

Moses said it first in the Old Testament: "I have set before you life and death, blessings and curses. Now choose life, so that you and your children may live…For the Lord is your life" (Deut. 30:19-20). Will you choose life, or death? The choice is yours.

If you want to choose your disease and choose your skepticism and all that ails you, fine. Choose it. But if you want to choose a miracle, then choose to release your faith. Choose the life of Jesus Christ. He will give you a new heart, a new mind, a new kidney, a new immune system— whatever you need—because he will give you a new life.

Prayer for your healing

Before we pray, I want to ask you one question. Do you really want to be healed? Think about that for a minute, and be honest. If you have been given a terminal diagnosis, the answer is obvious. But most people who do not suffer from a life-threatening disease need to ask themselves that question: Do I really want to be healed?

Without knowing it, some people cling to sickness because it is, as strange as it sounds, in some ways comforting. When you're sick, you have everyone's attention and concern. Maybe you feel more valuable as a person when you're sick because everyone sympathizes with you and pets you. Your self-esteem may be so low that you feel you don't deserve that kind of love and concern unless you're sick. Also, you're excused from doing a lot of things when you're sick. Could it be that you are avoiding responsibility by staying sick?

It's a sad fact that some people enjoy the worst of health. If they were healed, they wouldn't have anything to talk about. Does that describe you? Is your personality wrapped up in your sickness? Don't despair! Jesus can not only heal you of your physical sickness, he can heal you from your emotional sickness, and he can deliver you from the temptation to stay sick.

When Jesus healed the man at the pool of Bethesda, he first asked him, "Do you want to get well?" The sick man said, "Sir, I have no one to help me into the pool when the water is stirred. While I am trying to get in, someone else goes down ahead of me" (John 5:6-7). He was telling Jesus that he wanted desperately to be healed. He had been an invalid for thirty-eight years. Without anyone to help him, he was struggling to lower his crippled body into the pool when the angel stirred the water. Someone always beat him to it. But thirty-eight years of pain and suffering were wiped out when Jesus healed him.

The Great Physician is asking you today: Do you want to be made well? Will you be healed? Will you exercise faith that goes beyond the limit of your knowledge? Will you reach out and touch the hem of his garment and let him heal you and change you?

Start by praying this prayer.

Lord, I ask you to liberate me from all doubts, and from all fear, and from every kind of skepticism that would prevent me from experiencing the very best you have for me. I want to be healed, Lord, and I ask you in faith for my healing from _____. I accept the healing that Jesus Christ purchased for me at the cross of Calvary. Help me learn to live in your divine health. Let

*your Holy Spirit fill me now as I begin to receive
healing for my body, my mind and my emotions.*

Now, this is my prayer for you. Agree with me as you
read it.

*Heavenly Father, in the name of the Lord Jesus
Christ, I pray for every person who is reading this.
Right now, by the authority of Jesus' name and by
the authority of God's word, I release the healing
virtue of God to heal my friend's physical body. I
come against every kind of sickness and disease,
every ache and pain, every infirmity or illness
that afflicts this person. I rebuke sickness and
bind it in the name of Jesus. Every disease in this
body is now destroyed by the stripes Jesus bore for
our healing.*

*Lord, I pray for emotional healing. For those
who are overcome by fear or worry or depression,
I rebuke every doubt and anxiety in the name of
the Son of God. For those who are searching for
self-significance, let them find it in Jesus Christ,
the Prince of Glory. I ask the Holy Spirit, who is
the source of peace, to invade their hearts and
minds. Pull up every root of bitterness, erase from
their mind every horrible experience they've ever
had. Release them from every terror. Those things
that torment them at night, that they cannot get
rid of, that they cannot shake, in Jesus' name,
leave their body right now. Let every person who
prays this prayer with me feel the healing virtue
of the Lord Jesus Christ in their heart, soul, mind,
body and emotions, in Jesus' name. Amen.*

Chapter 5

Healing Through Deliverance

When you start talking about healing through deliverance, you'll stir up a hornet's nest of controversy.

Somehow it's all right for Hollywood to produce *Rosemary's Baby,* a movie where Satan has sexual intercourse with a woman and produces a living devil, or *The Exorcist,* a movie demonstrating the power of demons to control people. But if the church of Jesus Christ says that there is a real devil whose objective is to destroy you...that he is the commander of a highly-organized supernatural force of principalities and powers and angels and demons... if a preacher is brazen enough to imply that Satan is alive and at work in the church and, for God's sake, maybe in the church members, then that's really controversial.

I want you to know that it's not only a possibility, it's a genuine probability that the devil is at work in your church. There are two things that Satan hates. He hates to be exposed, and he hates to be expelled. God's word commands that the church do both. Jesus did it, and we're supposed to do it, too. The fact that we haven't done it, simply means that we're too cowardly to preach the gospel, and too weak to practice the gospel.

How very carnal we have made the church. We are supposed to be engaged in supernatural warfare. Instead we are worshipping the "trinity" of buildings, budgets and baptisms. The church promotes bazaars and book reviews, bingo and brotherhood barbeques. All of those things may have their place, but I want you to know that the devil is not afraid of a church who knows how to eat barbeque in the back yard. The devil is afraid of a church who knows how, through the authority of the name of Jesus and the blood of the cross, to expose him and expel him.

The reality of the destroyer

Begin with this fact: there is a very real devil, and his objective is to steal, kill and destroy (John 10:10). It was a very real devil that entered the Garden of Eden and seduced Adam and Eve to rebel against God. It was a very real devil that tempted Jesus in the wilderness. John the Revelator called him, "that old serpent, the devil" (Rev. 12:9).

In medieval theater, the devil was always presented as a mythological character, portrayed by someone in a red suit with horns and tail. That myth has survived until the 20th century. But the word of God exposes the devil for who he is, his personality, his method and his agenda.

Satan is not a myth. He is very real, and he wants to destroy your health. He wants to destroy your peace of mind. He wants to destroy your relationships. He wants to destroy your finances. He wants to destroy your marriage. He wants to control you and your emotions. He wants to enslave you by addictions. He wants you to be filled with bitterness and hatred and jealousy. He wants your whole life to be devastated.

The only protection we have from this monster is the authority of the name of Jesus, the word of God, and the blood of the cross. If you do not have Jesus Christ as your Savior and Lord, if you do not believe in the veracity of the word of God, if you do not believe in the power of the blood of Jesus Christ, you will be mastered by demon spirits.

What does the Bible say about Satan and his attempts

to control your life? The Bible says that Satan is a liar and the *father of all lies*; there is no truth in him (John 8:44). When you lie, you are being controlled by an evil spirit. When someone lies about you, they are doing the work of Satan. All liars shall have their part in the lake of fire (Rev. 21:8). There is no such thing as a "white lie" or a "little bitty lie." A "little bitty lie" will send you to a red-hot, great big hell.

Revelation 12:10 says Satan is the *accuser of the brethren*. When you accuse a brother or sister in Christ, you have become the devil's advocate. You are literally a satanic evangelist, ministering destruction to the life of another person.

Satan and his demons want to deceive you. The devil is the master of deception, and he loves to cast his deception in a religious light. He controls preachers who preach what Paul called "another gospel" (2 Cor. 11:4). Any gospel that tells you how to get to God the Father, or heaven, without Jesus Christ, is "another gospel." It's a counterfeit gospel, a living lie.

Everybody's preaching in the name of God today, but a lot of it has absolutely nothing to do with God. When you start mentioning the name of Jesus, you separate people who believe in God. Everbody all over the world believes in God. But God who? God is not some universal knowledge or energy force. He is God Almighty, the Father of Jesus Christ, the only name whereby men may be saved, and he is King of Kings and Lord of Lords. If the god you believe in does not have a son named Jesus Christ, then you are believing in the wrong god.

The Bible says Satan is such a master of deception that he can transform himself into an *angel of light* and can even present himself as a "minister of righteousness" (2 Cor. 11:14). A woman told me the story of her brother, who was dying from AIDS. One day she visited him in the hospital and he said, "Last night Jesus appeared to me." The woman looked at her brother's face and she could not see any peace. So she said, "The Jesus who appeared to you, did he have scars in his hands?" Although he was almost dead, her brother jumped up in the middle of the bed and began to curse violently. He had seen a radiant creature all right, but it was not Jesus Christ.

Every time I see another bestselling book by some pseudospiritual celebrity who says, "I've seen God," I want to ask them this: did you see the Son of God that had scars in his hands, or some luminous creature that was an agent from hell sent to destroy you with deception?

Your adversary, the devil, is also called a *roaring lion*, and he is portrayed as stalking the earth, seeking to devour the unsuspecting (1 Pet. 5:8). A lion controls by fear and intimidation, but if you know Jesus Christ, the Lion of the Tribe of Judah, you need not be afraid. Mention the name of Jesus Christ and demons tremble with fear. Mention that name and you have power over death, hell and the grave. Mention that name, because there is no other name given among men whereby we must be saved, other than the name of Jesus Christ (Acts 4:12). He is the Fairest of Ten Thousand, the Bread of Life, the Living Water. He is the Lion of the Tribe of Judah, the King of all Kings, the Lord of all Lords. And he is coming again with power and great glory to rule and reign on this earth, hallelujah!

The kingdom of the destroyer

The Bible says that Satan has a kingdom. In Matthew 12:25, Jesus said that every kingdom divided against itself cannot stand. "And if Satan cast out Satan, he is divided against himself; how shall then his kingdom stand?" (verse 26)

Note three things in this verse. First, Satan has a kingdom. Secondly, that kingdom is united under Satan's command. Thirdly, that kingdom has not been overthrown. That's right, it has not been overthrown. Jesus won our victory and defeated Satan at the cross, but his kingdom, with its principalities and powers, is still very much intact.

In Ephesians 6:12, Paul said that we are engaged in a life and death struggle with an enemy that is not physical but spiritual. "We are up against," Paul said, "unseen powers that control this dark world, and the spiritual agents from the very headquarters of sin, located in the heavenlies" (Phillips translation).

You are locked in a life and death struggle with a supernatural enemy who wants to destroy your health, your peace of mind, your marriage, your children, your business, your dreams and your aspirations, and if you don't know he exists or how to fight him, you will be killed by your ignorance.

That very statement irritates the powers and principalities that are trying to destroy you. Go back and read it again, because you may have "blanked out" while you were reading. See, that's how Satan works. He's into mind control. He tries to blind your eyes, "lest the light of the glorious gospel of Christ" shine on you and you be converted or delivered (2 Cor. 4:4).

Brilliant men can come to the house of God, hear a simple gospel sermon, and go home confused. They simply do not have the ability to absorb it because they lost a supernatural battle that happened while the word of God was going forth. That's happening to some of you right now who are reading this book. Satan wants to distract you and divert your mind because you're struggling to come into a dimension of healing and he wants to keep you sick.

God wants to bring you into a new dimension of liberty, a new dimension of peace. You're wrestling with the idea that there is something in your life not surrendered to Jesus Christ. Any area of your life not surrendered to Jesus Christ is under the control of the prince of darkness, and you need to get rid of it so that you can have the health, the healing, the peace and the power of the resurrected Son of God.

The destroyer has a kingdom peopled with evil spirits with demonic powers. Let's look at what the word of God says about these demonic capabilities and characteristics.

First of all, we see that *demons have a will*. In the fifth chapter of Mark, Jesus cast many demons out of the demoniac of Gadara. This was the only person Jesus ever met who was totally controlled by evil spirits. He lived in the cemetery, which was the asylum of his day for those who were insane, or beside themselves. Mark says they would bind him with chains, only to find the iron fetters broken and torn in pieces.

When the demons came out of him, they craved to inhabit a body. There was a large herd of swine grazing nearby, and the demons begged Jesus to send them into the herd of swine. We also see from this verse that *demons can speak*. Jesus granted the demons permission to enter the swine, and all 2,000 of them ran down the mountain and were drowned in the sea. That event should be in the Guinness Book for the biggest case of deviled hams on record!

Demons have a will. Demons can speak. And *demons have emotion*. James 2:19 says that demons "also believe and tremble." They tremble because they're afraid. Fear is an emotion. Demons believe in the power of God and it causes them to tremble.

Demons have supernatural knowledge. Mark 1:23 says there was a man with an unclean spirit in the synagogue where Jesus was teaching. The evil spirits cried out, "What have we to do with you, Jesus of Nazareth? Have you come to destroy us? We know who you are, the Holy One of God" (v. 24). The demons spoke. They were afraid Jesus would destroy them. And they knew supernaturally that Jesus was "the Holy One of God."

If you have a will, if you have intellect, if you have self-awareness and knowledge, you are, according to psychological principles, a person. The word of God shows that these supernatural beings, who are bent on your destruction, do exist.

Jesus came to destroy the destroyer

That verse in Mark says that the demons were afraid of Jesus. They asked him, "Have you come to destroy us?" The bad news for them, but the good news for you, is that that is exactly what Jesus came to do: destroy them.

Satan has a ministry of destruction, but so does Jesus. John 10:10 says the thief (Satan) comes "to steal, and to kill, and to *destroy*." But look at 1 John 3:8: "For this purpose the Son of God was manifested, that he might *destroy* the works of the devil." Jesus came to destroy the destroyer, and you can thwart any attack of Satan in the authority of the name of Jesus Christ!

Before I give you some tips on how you can recognize and destroy any demonic activity in your life, I want to share two personal experiences to show you how I was introduced to the reality of evil spirits in 1971.

Understand that I was raised in the home of Bible scholars. My father was an Assemblies of God pastor for 52 years. My mother was a Bible college instructor when she married my father. When I was growing up, we sat around the table and discussed the word of God, because that was uppermost in our thoughts.

But somehow I got the impression that the devil only operated in foreign countries where illiteracy and superstition were rampant. After all, I had degrees from three different universities and I was pastoring a church in a big city in the freest country on earth. Surely the devil wasn't at work in my church!

The behavior some of my members exhibited, however, could only be attributed to the devil. I'm not saying they were full of the devil, but they were acting like the devil. They had problems with their health, problems with their emotions, problems with their minds, and problems with their family relationships that no amount of counseling would help. After spending all those years in the university, and having been trained from my youth up in the scriptures, my secular education and my theology were locked in a mortal combat. That was when I prayed a dangerous prayer.

I said, "Lord, your word says 'if a man lacks wisdom, let him ask.' I'm asking you that if these people are ensnared in a spiritual dimension I'm not aware of [that's a nice phrase for evil spirits], I want you to show it to me. Hello and goodbye." That's how I prayed. Did the Lord ever enroll me quickly in the school of spiritual hard knocks.

My encounter with the demonized Presbyterian

The next morning I went to work as usual. The phone rang and a lady said, "Pastor Hagee, would you come to my home and pray for me? I have a demon spirit." Whoa! "Why did you use that word?" I asked her. "Well, maybe it was the wrong word," she said, "but I think that's what I've got." You could have knocked me over with a feather.

I asked her if she was a member of my church, and she said no, she was a Presbyterian. Whew! Thank God. I figured maybe Presbyterians could be demonized, but I was mainly just relieved that she wasn't in my church. So I said okay, I would come to her home.

This lady did not live in some thatched hut in a foreign country. She lived in a beautiful, spacious home in the good old United States of America. She was not illiterate, she was a college graduate. But she had been involved with Tarot cards and ouija boards for about 15 years.

"Last night," she told me, "I was sitting in my home alone. My husband was away on business. I heard the front door open, and then I heard something walk down the hall and walk into the room with me." I stopped her and said, "Some*thing* or some*one*?" She said, "No, some*thing*." I said, "You heard it, but you didn't see it?" She said, "That's right." I tell you, that lady had my attention.

She continued her story. "Then it walked into this room and it entered me." I said, "Wait a minute. How do you know it entered you?" In my mind, I'm ticking off all of the hours of abnormal psychology I had in graduate school, trying to find some label that would fit this lady. She said she knew it had entered her because her mind became filled with vicious, vulgar thoughts. She had begun to curse for no reason, and her mind had been filled with the most filthy, sexual things that could come to a human mind. "I just want to be free from this," she said.

"Well," I said, "let's do this just like we would a laboratory experiment. Jesus met a person in Luke 8 who had a similar problem. I'm just going to read the Bible story and we'll see what happens." She said, "Fine," and I began to read Luke 8 where Jesus cast the evil spirit out of the demoniac of Gadara. As I read the story I looked over at the lady, and my eyes could have popped out of my head. She was a slender lady, sitting on the sofa so poised and sophisticated. All of a sudden she reached down and grabbed her ankles and brought her feet up over her head, and with her head nearly touching the floor she began to hiss like a snake.

I felt like saying, "Lady, where would you like the new door to be in your house, because I'm getting ready to run straight through that brick wall!" But I decided to stick with the program, so I went back to Luke 8. I saw where Jesus spoke directly to the evil spirit in the demoniac of Gadara, so I said to the lady, "In the name of Jesus Christ, I command the evil power to come out of you." I didn't shout or get emotional, I just said it in a normal tone of voice. And in the deepest, most masculine voice, which was obviously not hers, she said, "I hate you, John Hagee."

Wow! It takes most people a while to hate me, but she hated me instantly! I really wanted to leave but knew I couldn't, what with a demonized contortionist twisted like a mongoose around a pole. Besides, I could sense there was some sort of contest going on here, and if there's one thing I like, it's a good fight. So I leaped into the fray. "In the name of Jesus Christ, the Son of the Living God, I command you to come out of this woman," I said in a stronger voice. The battle raged for about forty-five minutes until she finally unwound herself and said, "It's left me. I'm free." She had been totally set free from that evil spirit by the power of Jesus Christ.

Her husband walked in about that time. He didn't believe in demon spirits—period. He checked his wife into a psychiatric hospital and had her examined for a week. The doctors finally said to just take her home, because there was nothing wrong with her mental health.

"Beg for your life, preacher"

Did you ever have one of those days that was just too exciting? When I got home that night after my encounter with the demonized Presbyterian, I got a phone call from one of my church members. God must have known that I was so hard-headed I would just rationalize that experience away, so he had round two ready.

This church member said, "Pastor, I just got a phone call from a man who said he was going to kill me. He's going to shoot me tomorrow." Here was somebody who needed me to scrape him off the ceiling, and I felt like I was up there myself. Well, I agreed to meet with the church member and his would-be murderer, and the next night they came to my office.

The man who was threatening murder was heavily into witchcraft. He sat right there in my office and said, "I worship the devil. And I have power from him." He claimed he could control people and money and circumstances through voodoo, and said he got his instructions every morning from a witch in California.

I asked him, "Would you like to be free to know the real power of the Lord Jesus Christ and the authority of his word?" He said, "No. I hate God. I hate God's word. And I hate you." It seemed like I was offending people left and right! The man stood up and started cursing me. He said, "I'm leaving, but you haven't seen the last of me."

He kept his word. The next Wednesday night he showed

up in church carrying a hand gun. He grabbed a church member from behind and marched him up the aisle at gunpoint. People were screaming and diving under pews. Some were crawling out of the church on their hands and knees. And some were praying, thank God.

About ten feet away from the pulpit, he stopped and pointed the gun at me and the man standing on the platform with me. "Beg for your life, preacher," he said, "because I'm going to shoot you both." I said, "Jesus is Lord here and I'm in authority, not you. The word of God says that no weapon formed against me shall prosper. I'm God's man in God's house and I'm not begging you or anybody else."

"On the count of three, I'm going to shoot you," he said. This time he lied. He started shooting on the count of two and emptied the gun. Although the shots were fired at virtually point blank range, not one bullet found its mark. When it was all over, he was arrested and sent to the hospital for the criminally insane. Ninety days later he was released and pronounced cured by the psychiatrists. The first day he was out, he climbed a tree and hung himself—because Satan is a murderer and a liar from the beginning and his desire is to rob you, destroy you and kill you.

At the end of that eventful week, I told the Lord that I was convinced there were evil spirits, they do control people, and he does want them cast out. I have been faithful to do so for twenty years now.

How to recognize demonic activity in your life

Okay, you recognize that there are evil spirits who wage war against you in the heavenlies. So how do you tell if there are any demonic influences operating in your life?

The general rule is that any area of your life that is compulsive or out of control, if you feel driven in any area, you're probably dealing with an evil spirit. Satan drives his people, but Jesus Christ is the Prince of Peace. Isaiah said the wicked are "like the tossing sea, which cannot rest" (57:20). When you can't rest, when your behavior is compulsive and it controls you, you're not talking about being controlled by the Holy Spirit.

Let's look at demonic activity in your emotional life. All of us have emotions, and we feel various kinds of emotions at various times. Sometimes we feel happy, sometimes we feel sad, sometimes we feel angry, sometimes we worry. That's normal. But when your emotions are constantly out of control, you need to look for a spiritual reason for your emotional turmoil.

If you have an unnatural fear that destroys your peace of mind, you are being tormented by an evil spirit. One of the worst things parents can do is to allow their children to watch horror shows on television. I don't know how many children I have had to pray for because their parents allowed them to watch horror shows and their minds became obsessed with some monster that was going to get them. Parents, you are allowing your children's minds to be opened to evil spirits when you let them watch ghostly garbage on television.

Don't think you're immune from demonic influence in this area because you're an adult, though. When you read Stephen King stories until late in the night, when you go see slasher movies like *Friday the 13th* and *Nightmare on Elm Street,* you're feeding your emotions with fear and not faith. God's not going to send you to hell for watching scary movies, but it makes it harder for you to receive God's peaceful sleep and rest when you've been feeding your emotions on nightmarish nonsense.

An unnatural fear of people, unnatural fear of death, unnatural fear of sickness, unnatural fear of the past or the future, an unnatural fear of failure—these fears are not from God. 2 Timothy 1:7 says "God has not given us the spirit of fear; but of power, and of love, and of a sound mind." So who gives you an unnatural fear? If it doesn't come from God, it can only come from the devil.

All of us get depressed now and then, and there are medical reasons for certain depressions. But if you are suffering from a depression that seems unbreakable, especially if either one of your parents was depressed, you are dealing with a demonic influence. When depression hangs over you like a cloud, when thoughts of suicide enter your mind, it's nothing more than an evil spirit trying to destroy you, because Satan is a murderer. Jesus can break the yoke of your depression and give you a dose of joy unspeakable in place of your spirit of heaviness.

Hatred is another type of demonic influence on your emotional life. Hatred of any kind is an expression of an evil spirit, because God is love. The hatred we see manifested most often is racial hatred. If you hate black people, white people, brown people, yellow people, red people, Jewish people, German people, Japanese people—if you hate anybody, you are controlled by an evil spirit. Satan wants the human race to divide itself and fight and devour each other like packs of dogs. Satan hates all of us, but God loves all of us. You'd better get on God's side and love everybody!

Other areas of demonic activity include emotional scenes that you constantly replay in your mind. A deep-seated bitterness against your mother, your father, a friend that has offended you—when you can't forget it and you constantly think about it, that does not come from God. You need to be freed from that by the power of the Lord.

Compulsive worry. Feelings of rejection. Total lack of confidence and massive insecurity. I want you to know something. You are a child of God. You are created a little lower than the angels. The royal blood of heaven flows in your veins. God did not manufacture a piece of junk when he manufactured you. You are somebody. God loves you. You are special. Lift up your head and rejoice. Live your life with joy because God lives in you through Jesus Christ.

Evil spirits can influence your thought life as well as your emotional life. Unbelief is the by-product of an evil spirit. The Bible says, "Without faith it is impossible to please God" (Heb. 11:6).

You say, "Preacher, if everybody who doesn't have faith is on God's blacklist, that's a lot of people." Yes, it is. But consider this verse in Revelation 21: "But the fearful, and unbelieving, and the abominable, and murderers, and whoremongers, and sorcerers, and idolators, and all liars, shall have their part in the lake [of fire]." This is not a good list, and God starts it off by saying that the fearful and the unbelieving will be those people who will live forever, by God's command, in the place called hell.

What is unbelief? It is a spirit that is skeptical of every move of God. Unbelief criticizes and belittles every move of the Holy Spirit. Unbelief kills revival fire in the church. Unbelief spreads the virus of doubt. Unbelief is straight out of hell and its purpose is to destroy the miracle mentality God intended for us to have.

Doubt, indecision, and procrastination can all be caused by demonic influences in your thought life. The Bible says "now is the day of salvation" (2 Cor. 6:2). King Agrippa told Paul, "Almost thou persuadest me to be a Christian" (Acts 26:28). When you're always putting God off, always saying you'll serve God when you have more time, when it's more convenient, when you're older—you're being influenced by demonic forces.

One of the most common areas of demonic influence in your thought life, even for some church members, is pornography and perversion. That's fueled by evil spirits. Many men are addicted to pornographic magazines. You can find them at just about every convenience store. You can even have them mailed to your home or office in a plain brown wrapper. But when you are addicted to pornography, you cannot have an honest sexual relationship with your wife, because what happens in the theater of your mind is far more exciting than what happens in your bedroom. You need to get that filth out of your mind, get it out of your marriage, and get it out of your mailbox. It's not art, it's trash. And it has no place in your home.

If you are driven to commit adultery or fornication, you

have yielded to an evil spirit. If you are driven to homosexual relationships, you are under demonic influence. Sex is to be confined to one man and one woman in a marriage relationship. Any other relationship is wrong. If your sexual relationships are not motivated by the Holy Spirit, then they are motivated by hellish spirits. You need to be free from the spirits that are driving you to destroy your marriage and your life.

If you have thoughts of revenge and murder, you are being driven by an evil spirit. Suicide is an evil spirit. Every kind of addiction is fueled by evil spirits—illegal drugs, legal drugs, alcohol, tobacco. Any substance that controls you does not come from God, it is straight out of hell. The Holy Spirit will not motivate you to fry your mind on any drug that will destroy your body and reduce you to a burned-out shell looking for a grave to fall into. The Holy Spirit will not help you organize your life around creative ways to drink. The Holy Spirit will not encourage you to poison your lungs one puff at a time.

If you have a vindictive, critical spirit, you have the living devil in you. Demonic activity in your speech brings forth lying, gossip, slander and tale bearing. The Bible says that life and death is in the tongue, so watch what you say. David said, "Lord, set a watch over my mouth" (Psalm 141:3). When you say something negative or hateful about another person, you have, fundamentally, cursed that person.

When you tell your son or daughter, "You're dumb. You can't learn. You'll never amount to anything," you have spoken a curse on the life of that child. It is a supernatural curse that can destroy them. Stop speaking curses on your children. Speak life into your son. Speak hope into your daughter. Speak inspiration into them. Speak the love of God into them.

Demonic activity in the spirit world

One of the most popular movies of the last few years is *Ghost*. The movie is a romantic comedy about a dead man who communicates with his wife through a medium. Americans see that premise presented in a laughable, funny kind of way, but they'll go right out and try it. And the moment they do, they open their minds and their lives to demonic invasion. They've been had, and don't even know how or why.

There has been a surge in the number of movies coming out that exploit the supernatural on the negative side: witches and demons, 666 and the antichrist and that spirit that is pervasive in the earth. Most people recognize that witchcraft and satanism are demonic practices, but so are fortune-telling, clairvoyance, mind control, ESP and other paranormal psychological phenomena, Tarot cards, ouija boards, and a whole host of other supernatural "tools for enlightenment." When you would rather read tea leaves or Tarot cards than the word of God for guidance, you have been duped and deceived.

The word of God says in Deuteronomy 19:10-12 that these people are an abomination to God: those who offer their children as sacrifices, those who practice divination or sorcery, those who interpret omens or "observe the times," enchanters and witches, those with a "familiar spirit" (a medium or spiritist), and necromancers (those who consult the dead).

An enchanter sounds like some ancient wizard, something we wouldn't have to worry about today. But an enchanter is actually someone who uses incantations or music to control people. Now does that begin to sound familiar to you? Right now, multiplied millions of our teenagers are being controlled with acid rock music. They sing lyrics that promote drug abuse, sexual violence and suicide, and then we wonder why they go out and do those things. You helped them do it by allowing them to listen to that kind of music.

A lot of you will say, "Well, I don't do any of those things," but you read your horoscope in the newspaper faithfully. When you read Jeanne Dixon or any other astrological prognosticator what you're saying is, "I'm looking to the occult to give me leadership for my life and not the word of God." The Bible says, "In all thy ways acknowledge him, and he shall direct thy paths" (Prov. 3:6). But when you turn to the occult or to horoscopes, you're turning your back on God and the leadership of the Holy Spirit.

Let me show you where that's found in the word of God and what it says will happen to those who dabble in the occult:

> *Disaster will come upon you, and you will not know how to conjure it away. A calamity will fall upon you that you cannot ward off with a ransom; a catastrophe you cannot foresee will suddenly come upon you. Keep on, then, with your magic spells and with your many sorceries, which you have labored at since childhood. Perhaps you will succeed, perhaps you will cause terror. All the counsel you have received has only worn you out! Let your astrologers come forward, those stargazers who make predictions month by month [Jeanne Dixon and company], let them save you from what is coming upon you. Surely they are like stubble; the fire will burn them up. They cannot even save themselves from the power of the flame... Each of them goes on in his error; there is not one that can save you..*

Isaiah 47:11-15, NIV

I won't take time to delve into the current popularity of the New Age movement. It's something you need to be informed about, though, because so much of this "new" philosophy and practice is rooted in the most ancient of evil.

Prayer for your deliverance

If there is any area of your life that is compulsive or out of control, you need to be set free from the supernatural forces that are driving you. You can't just "think free" and be free. Only Jesus can set you free.

You have the opportunity right now to choose between life and death, between liberty and bondage. Some people will choose to continue in bondage because they don't want to admit there's an area of their life that's under the control of demonic influence. But if you really want to be free, you can be. How do you get free?

First of all, admit that you need to be set free. Secondly, ask God to forgive you of all known sin. Thirdly, forgive everyone who has ever hurt you. If you don't forgive others, God cannot forgive you. Then call upon the name of the Lord as Deliverer, and the chains will be broken instantaneously, miraculously, by the authority of his name, the power of his blood, and the authority of his word. It's not emotion or magic. It is the supernatural power of the resurrected Son of God, Jesus Christ—the real Jesus, the one with scars in his hands.

Pray this prayer out loud now.

> *Lord, I ask you now to forgive me for all the sin in my life. Cleanse me by the blood of Jesus Christ. I ask you now, Lord, to give me the power to forgive everyone who has hurt me. Help me now to forgive _____ for _____ (mention their name and the circumstance). I have been hurt deeply and can't get over it, but I confess it now in Jesus' name.*
>
> *I have asked you to forgive me of my sins. I have forgiven others. Now I call upon you as my deliverer. Your word says that whoever calls on the name of the Lord will be delivered. I ask you, Jesus Christ, by your shed blood, to deliver me now from _____. Thank you, Jesus,*

for your delivering power, and thank you, Holy Spirit, for helping me to receive my deliverance, in Jesus' name. Amen.

Now, this is my prayer for you. Agree with me as you read it.

In the name of the Lord Jesus Christ, I bind those evil spirits that control our emotions. I bind every kind of resentment and every form of hatred...every kind of bitterness and rejection... every kind of compulsive worry and insecurity and depression. I command it to go in the name of the Lord Jesus Christ. Leave the body of Christ, for we are the sons and daughters of God.

In the name of the Lord Jesus Christ, I come against every evil spirit that affects our thought life. I bind every thought of self pity and suicide...every thought of murder and revenge... every thought of perversion and pornography. I command these thoughts to go in the name of Jesus Christ. I come against every area of sexual impurity...those who are driven by adultery... those who are driven by fornication... those who are driven by homosexuality...those who are driven by incest. I break those roots out of the body of Christ and out of our minds.

Evil spirits, I command you in the name of the son of God, leave this person alone, because Jesus Christ is Lord. I come against the spirit of witch-craft in Jesus' name. I come against astrology and horoscopes and fortune telling. I command these spirits to leave and I root them out by the authority of the name of Jesus and the power of his blood. Be set free, in Jesus' name. Hallelujah.

Now take time to bless the Lord and thank him for your deliverance.

Chapter 6

Fasting and Praying for Miracle-Working Power

Our generation is fascinated with power. You no longer get dressed for work in the morning, you power dress. You no longer go out to lunch with a business associate, you have a power lunch. You no longer have conversations, you have power talks. My father and I had a few of those power talks when I was a boy. I remember all the power coming in my direction, however.

Our gospel is a gospel of power. Jesus said, "All power is given unto me in heaven and in earth" (Matt. 28:18). He gave that power first to his disciples, and, by extension, to his church. Power over disease and over demon spirits. Power over death and over hell and over the grave. Power over principalities and power in the heavenlies.

When you believe, you have power. The Bible says that to those who believe, he gave power to become the sons of God (John 1:12). Acts 1:8 says, "You shall receive power, after that the Holy Ghost is come upon you." We pray the Lord's prayer: "For thine is the kingdom, and the power, and the glory forever."

We have the power that can deliver you from sickness and disease, from drugs and alcohol, from depression and despair. That power can give you supernatural protection from harm and danger. How do you receive this miracle-working power? It's yours through fasting and prayer.

Let's look at a very special story in the 17th chapter of Matthew:

> *There came to him a certain man, kneeling down to him, and saying, Lord, have mercy on my son: for he is lunatic, and sore vexed: for ofttimes he falleth into the fire, and oft into the water. And I brought him to thy disciples, and they could not cure him. Then Jesus answered and said, O faithless and perverse generation, how long shall I be with you? how long shall I suffer you? bring him hither to me. And Jesus rebuked the devil; and he departed out of him: and the child was cured from that very hour. Then came the disciples to Jesus apart, and said, Why could not we cast him out? And Jesus said unto them, Because of your unbelief: for verily I say unto you, If ye have faith as a grain of mustard seed, ye shall say unto this mountain, Remove hence to yonder place; and it shall remove; and nothing shall be impossible unto you. Howbeit, this kind goeth not out but by prayer and fasting.*
>
> Matthew 17:14-21

A father has a son so possessed by the devil that the demon spirits are throwing him into the fire, trying to burn him, and into the water, trying to drown him. The father brought the child to the disciples, but they were powerless to help the boy. Then the father took his son to Jesus Christ, who delivered him instantly. Jesus rebuked the disciples and told them that this kind only comes out by fasting and prayer. Jesus was saying this: there is a dimension in the supernatural where you reach the ultimate power only through fasting and prayer.

In this story is the portrait of the church today. There are many great needs, but there is either not enough power, or no power at all, to meet those needs. The world is looking for the power of God. We have it and we can make it available through fasting and prayer.

Yet mention fasting to the average church congregation and faces will fall, heads will shake and hands will tremble. Fasting is just about as exciting to most Christians as going to the dentist for a root canal. I could get more people to volunteer for an IRS audit than to fast and pray.

What King Stomach has done to humanity

Fasting is not a pleasant experience, because it crucifies King Stomach. Women know that the quickest way to a man's heart is through his stomach. Satan knows that, too. Just look at the Bible and you'll see what King Stomach has done to humanity. Eve came to Adam with an apple. He took one bite of it and they ate us out of a house and home.

The three sins of Sodom and Gomorrah were homosexuality, drunkenness and gluttony. Gluttony means excessive eating. When you stand on the bathroom scales and the springs explode out the side, it's time for you to prayerfully consider fasting.

Esau sold his entire future, called his birthright, down the drain for one bowl of red beans. He destroyed his whole life because he could not control King Stomach.

The children of Israel bellyached for forty years because God gave them manna to eat. He fed them every day with the most nutritious food imaginable, and they still complained. Exodus 16:3 records their complaint: "Would to God we had died by the hand of the Lord in the land of Egypt, when we sat by the flesh pots, and when we did eat bread to the full; for ye have brought us forth into this wilderness, to kill this whole assembly with hunger."

God delivered them when they were being beaten and killed in Egypt, yet here they are romanticizing about what a great life they had in Egypt sitting around pots of meat. They bellyached about God's feeding them manna until he said, "All right. You want meat, I'll give you meat." Psalm 78 tells the story of how God sent a strong wind that blew in millions of fowl, so many they could knock them out of the air with their hands. They prepared their long-awaited meal of meat, and the Bible says that while the meat was in their mouths, God killed them.

There are a couple of things you want to learn from this story. First, don't criticize the cooking! Secondly, when God is providing for you, rejoice and be exceedingly glad, because he is very sensitive about people who murmur about what he is doing. Thirdly, Satan knows that fasting releases God's power, and he does not want you to discover how to be a powerful Christian. He doesn't mind if you sing a little bit and give a dollar or two every week. But if you really learn how to be a powerful Christian, the devil is in trouble as far as controlling your life is concerned.

When Jesus was in the wilderness fasting, Satan tempted him with turning stones into bread. Why? He wanted Jesus to give in to the carnal flesh and break the fast. He knew that when Jesus came out of the wilderness at the end of this fast, he would be filled with the power of God. That's exactly what happened. Jesus did not break his fast, and when he came out of the wilderness, the first thing he did was hold a healing service. People from three different nations were supernaturally healed in such numbers that his fame spread by word of mouth throughout the entire region. Jesus had a power from God they had never seen before. If you would like to experience the power of God in a dimension you have never known in all of your life, begin to fast and pray.

Three kinds of fasting

What is fasting? It is not dieting in Jesus' name. Fasting is doing without food, at God's direction, for spiritual purposes and spiritual power. Fasting is not something fanatics do. Fasting is not for the superreligious. It is to be a normal part of the Christian life.

Jesus is our example and he fasted on one occasion for forty days, and for one day on numerous occasions. All the disciples fasted. Paul and the other apostles fasted. Moses and Joshua both fasted for forty days, and they weren't even charismatics! Elijah fasted for forty days. Daniel fasted for 21 days. The entire nation of Israel fasted for three days and nights for deliverance from an Old Testament Hitler by the name of Haman. These people changed the course of history by fasting and prayer.

Prayer and fasting is to be a normal part of a New Testament believer's life. Look at three verses from Matthew chapter 6. Matthew 6:2, *when* you give alms, not if you give alms. Matthew 6:5, *when* you pray, not if you pray. Matthew 6:16, *when* you fast, not if you fast.

Although fasting is to be a normal part of our spiritual life, we are not to call attention to our fasting. That's what the Pharisees did, they fasted for recognition. They stood on the street corner with long faces and sad eyes. They wanted their hollow, haggard looks to cause people to say, "Oh, he's so holy." Their descendants are in the charismatic movement today. One of them will stand up in a testimony service and say, "I just want to testify to the glory of God that I have missed three boxes of the Colonel's fried chicken, two chocolate malts and a supreme pizza, all for the kingdom, of course."

There are three kinds of fasting in the Bible: a normal fast, an absolute fast, and a partial fast. A normal fast is doing without food for a specific time to achieve a specific purpose.

Then there is an absolute fast, which is doing without food *and* water. I don't recommend you do without water unless God sovereignly tells you to do so, because it can be dangerous to your health. Paul had an absolute fast in Acts 9:9, probably because he was in absolute shock. He had just been knocked off his horse on the Damascus road, he had completely lost his sight, and God had his undivided attention. God spoke to him while he was fasting and told him what to do to be healed.

There is also a partial fast, which is doing without desserts or rich foods. A partial fast is not fasting from midnight until daylight. A partial fast does not include eating breakfast and lunch like a hog so you can coast through supper with an Alka Seltzer.

An example of a partial fast is found in the first chapter of Daniel. The three Hebrew children put themselves on a partial fast when they were in Babylonian captivity. They refused the king's rich food and his wine, not to be obnoxious, but because the food had been offered to idols. They asked for the normal, bland diet of the Jewish community, and they flourished on it, to the amazement of their captors.

The benefits of fasting

What are the benefits of fasting? First of all, it purifies your body, sort of like a physical spring cleaning. Secondly, fasting brings power. Jesus was led into the wilderness by the Holy Spirit. He fasted for 40 days and came out with so much power that he shook nations in one day. It is better to preach with power for one day than to bore humanity for 40 years with a humdrum ministry.

Thirdly, fasting brings protection. In the book of Ezra we find that Hezekiah declared a fast for protection from thieves as they transported the silver and gold to the house of God. A fourth benefit of fasting is the release of spiritual gifts. Paul fasted and prayed that spiritual gifts would be manifested in his life.

A fifth benefit to fasting is deliverance from evil spirits and addictive habits. Deliverance is going to be *the* ministry between now and the rapture of the church. Why? Because we have a generation of young people listening to rock music and opening their minds and bodies to a supernatural invasion. They are being infested and infected with demonic spirits and once that spirit takes them over, they need deliverance. We have a generation of adults who are seeking spiritual experiences in New Age crystals and metaphysical manifestations. When they go to a liturgical church that knows nothing more about God than singing a hymn and reading a Bible verse and going home, they will not be changed. The only thing that can turn them around is the supernatural power of the Holy Spirit setting them free.

Isaiah 58:6 says that the fast the Lord has chosen is "to loose the bands of wickedness, to undo the heavy burdens, and to let the oppressed go free and that you break every yoke." The oppressed means the slaves. You break the yoke of slavery through fasting and prayer. Is your child a slave to drugs? Fasting and prayer can break that yoke. Are you a slave to alcohol or tobacco? Fasting and prayer can break that yoke. Those who are slaves to cults, slaves to rock music, slaves to witchcraft—all those who are oppressed can go free when every yoke is broken through fasting and prayer.

Another benefit of fasting is guidance. My grandfather had ten sons. One time the next to youngest, Joel Lavon, jumped out of a tree into a dry creek bed and drove a stob into his foot. His leg began to swell and the doctors said it was blood poisoning. The only thing they could do to save his life was to cut his leg off, so they scheduled it for the next morning.

My grandfather, who was a man of prayer, began to intercede and asked God to show him what was wrong with his son's leg. After several hours of prayer, he got up and said, "God has shown me that there is a plug of moss in his foot. If I get that plug of moss out, his leg will be spared." He got a crochet hook from my grandmother and thrust it into boy's foot. When he pulled it out, there came that plug of moss, and behind it all of the corruption that was causing the blood poisoning.

Within hours his leg had returned to normal. Instead of losing his leg, he was up and running around in two days—

because God can show you what you need to know, when you need to know it, for the preservation of your family, if you'll ask with prayer and fasting.

There is a kind of healing that goes into another dimension, and it only happens with fasting and praying.

My oldest brother had grand mal epilepsy manifested by absolutely horrible seizures. My mother declared she would fast and pray until God healed her boy. We took him to doctors and they couldn't stop the seizures. We took him to every faith healing ministry in America. Nothing happened. My mother continued to fast and pray for three years. One Wednesday night she prayed for my brother. When she touched him that night, he dropped to the floor like he had been shot. He was supernaturally healed on the spot, and from that day until this one has enjoyed ridiculously good health—because God will do the impossible for you if you'll fast and pray.

Chapter 7

We Are Fasting and Praying for Your Miracle

So far I have shared with you several incidents of healing in my family. These healings were all the result of prayer and fasting. I want to share with you now how our entire church body has been led to fast and pray corporately for miracles of healing in our congregation and in our television audience around the world.

When individuals fast and pray it releases the power of God in their lives in a new dimension. When you fast and pray corporately, as a church, as the unified body of Christ, the power of God is unleashed against Satan's principalities and powers to a degree you can scarcely imagine.

A biblical example of corporate fasting and prayer

Fasting and prayer will destroy Satan's attack on God's people and frustrate the armies of hell.

2 Chronicles 20:3 says that when messengers came to tell Jehoshaphat that the armies of three nations were arrayed against Judah, he proclaimed a fast for the entire nation. All the people of Judah came together to seek the Lord—all the men, with their wives and children, stood before the Lord as one body, asking for his divine intervention. As they fasted and prayed, the spirit of the Lord came

upon one of the musicians, named Jahaziel, and he began to prophesy. This is what he said:

> *Listen, King Jehoshaphat and all who live in Judah and Jerusalem! This is what the Lord says to you: "Do not be afraid or discouraged because of this vast army. For the battle is not yours, but God's. Tomorrow march down against them. They will be climbing up by the Pass of Ziz, and you will find them at the end of the gorge in the Desert of Jeruel. You will not have to fight this battle. Take up your positions; stand firm and see the deliverance the Lord will give you, O Judah and Jerusalem. Do not be afraid; do not be discouraged. Go out to face them tomorrow, and the Lord will be with you."*
>
> 2 Chronicles 20:15-17

At this word, Jehoshaphat and all the people fell down and worshipped God. Then the choir stood up and began to praise the Lord with loud voices. Jehoshaphat consulted with the people and they made a corporate decision to send the choir out ahead of the army—don't you know that would thrill your music minister!

The Lord had told them exactly where the enemy would be, and that's where the choir and army of Judah took up their positions. When the enemy started climbing up that hill by the Pass of Ziz they ran smack-dab into a troop of Holy Ghost anointed singers who had fasted and prayed until they could face the legions of hell armed only with the weapons of praise and thanksgiving. When they started singing, "Praise the Lord, for his mercy endures forever," I want you to know the devil and his demons couldn't get out of that valley fast enough. The armies of Ammon and Moab began to kill the army from Mount Seir. When they finished slaughtering the men from Seir, they turned and destroyed one another. It happened exactly as the Lord had revealed to them during their fast—they did not have to fight.

I could preach a month of sermons on that one chapter, but I only want to make one point here: God's supernatural power was released in an unprecedented way because the entire nation came together in corporate fasting and prayer. Fasting and prayer is still God's way of waging supernatural warfare. It will work in your family and in your church just like it worked for the nation of Israel. As a boy I saw it work in my father's church, and I can tell you that it is working in Cornerstone Church now.

God still works miracles when the church fasts and prays

During the second World War, my father had seventeen Marines in his church. All of them went through Guadalcanal and Iwo Jima. Some of them were in groups where the mortality rate was 90%. There was someone in our church, every day of the war, from the day after Pearl Harbor until victory came, fasting and praying for the protection of those seventeen men. I can testify to the glory of God that all seventeen of them came home. Most of them came home wounded. One of them came home without an arm. But they all came home alive, because God can protect you in the worst of circumstances.

Last year our church was called to fast and pray when Lizzy Gross, the ten-year-old daughter of our music minister, John Gross, was stricken with a brain tumor. Her left eye had begun to drift to the outside and she was seeing double. The first doctor they took her to said it could be corrected with minor surgery. But when her eye began to drift further to the outside, Lizzy's parents became alarmed and took her to see a specialist. This doctor said that Lizzy either had multiple sclerosis, myasthenia gravis, or a brain tumor, and that an MRI would be required to make a definite diagnosis.

The MRI showed conclusively that Lizzy had a tumor in the center of her brain. Because of its location, it could not be operated on, nor was there any treatment for it. Her medical death sentence was pronounced by the finest medical minds in San Antonio. They said that as the tumor grew her vision would deteriorate further and she would have horrible headaches. She was given about a year to live.

It was a declaration the membership of Cornerstone Church refused to accept. I called on our 10,000-plus members to declare every Monday a day of fasting and prayer for Lizzy's healing. Our church came together with a demonstration of fasting and prayer seldom seen. A spiritual army began to put on the whole armor of God, and the fight for Lizzy's life was on.

The symptoms predicted by the doctor began to come to pass exactly as they had said. Lizzy's left eye became completely turned outside so that she lost the use of that eye. Her eyelids drooped. Her headaches grew worse. We paid no attention to the physical symptoms because we were reaching into the supernatural realm for a miracle from God. We chose to believe the biblical report and not the medical report.

John came into my study early one morning. He was obviously shaken. The school had called and said to come pick Lizzy up because she was having a terrible headache. She was in so much pain she could not stay in class. John knew that these headaches were what the doctor said would happen when the tumor began to grow.

I told him, "John, we are standing on the word of God. We have met God's conditions for a miracle and your daughter will live and not die. Go pick up Lizzy, take her home, and put her to bed like it was a sinus headache. Rebuke this fear that is trying to strangle this miracle."

That's exactly what John did. Lizzy was put to bed. The next morning her parents noticed that her left eye had dramatically improved. They waited a few days and her eye kept getting better. They finally took her back for another MRI, and this MRI confirmed that the tumor was gone. Lizzy had been completely healed by the power of

God released through prayer and fasting.

Word of Lizzy's healing began to spread. Her testimony was shared on the 700 Club and Trinity Broadcasting Network, in *Charisma* magazine, and through other avenues. As the news of Lizzy's healing spread, we began to get phone calls from all over the country asking for prayer. We have added additional volunteers to handle the calls to our Lifeline Telephone Center, but on Sundays our phone lines are still sometimes jammed. People with desperate needs are calling and asking us to pray for a miracle. And as we continue to fast and pray on Mondays, we are seeing dramatic evidences of God's miracle-working power.

We will fast and pray until you receive your miracle

We want to help you receive a miracle, too. Let us know your prayer requests and we will take them to the throne of grace. We will fast and pray until you receive your miracle.

Someone asked me recently, "Will you really pray for my request, or are you just adding my name to your computer?" Let me tell you, we pray for every prayer request. And if you want to receive our newsletter or catalog, we'll add your name to our computer. But you don't even have to give your full name or address when you call.

Your call will be answered by a volunteer who is an anointed prayer warrior. He or she will pray with you on the spot. Each prayer request is written down and brought to our daily prayer meetings where we lay hands on them and pray together. We take every request as seriously as if it were for our own family—because God's family is our family.

This miracle prayer ministry is a calling from God, a divine commission of intercession. Our volunteers have told me that weeks later they will still be thinking about a particular call they have received, and as the Holy Spirit brings that person to their mind, they continue to pray for their need.

If you are believing for a miracle from God, call or write and let us know. We will fast and pray with you. We will take up our position with you at the place of battle God has revealed to us. And when the enemy tries to cross those battle lines, he'll have to face an entire army of spiritual warriors operating in the miracle dimension of fasting and prayer.

John Hagee Ministries
PO Box 1400
San Antonio, TX 78295

Lifeline Telephone Center
(512) 491-5100
Monday–Friday 8:00 a.m. to 11:00 p.m.
Sunday 6:00 a.m. until 11:00 p.m.
Central Time

Chapter 8

The Cassette Tape Miracle

In chapter two we looked at the importance of the word of God in receiving your miracle. There is no greater illustration of this than the miracle of healing experienced by my uncle, Joel Lavon Hagee, a retired minister who presently lives in Oceanside, California. Here is his testimony, in his own words, as he shared it in one of our church services recently.

It is a real joy to give this testimony of what Jesus has done and the miracle he has given me. I want you to know that miracles do not happen just by wanting them to happen. You have to lay the ground work for them.

Before I tell you my testimony, I want to assure you that I was rooted and grounded in the word of God. From 1975 to 1981 I had read the Bible through forty times. I had read the New Testament an additional 80 times. I was in the word of God daily. I was living in the word, and I do live in the word to this day. You'll understand what I mean when I finish my testimony.

My wife found me dead

On April 18, 1981, at approximately 10:00 in the morning, my wife found me dead. The doctors don't know how long I was dead, but my body had already mottled, my veins had collapsed, my eyes were turned back, my mouth was open, and I was a very ugly spectacle. When my wife found me dead, she thought if she would slap my face (what a privilege she took!), it would bring me back to my senses. It didn't work. But she did begin to speak in faith. If the word of God is in you, you can speak in faith. She said out loud, "You will not die. You are not going to die." As an afterthought she added, "You're not going to leave me in this mess!"

She called Amcare, and there was a fire department two blocks from my house, so the paramedics got there quickly and began to work on me. While this was happening, two phone calls were made. My sister-in-law felt impressed of the Holy Spirit to slip out of a prayer meeting and phone her mother, who lived two doors down from us. She asked her mother, "What's wrong? There's something wrong. I can feel it." Her mother said, "Yes, Lavon has had a heart attack. They're trying to resuscitate him right now." She ran back into that Full Gospel Businessmen's meeting and they began to pray. God had planned it that this would glorify his name, hallelujah!

The second phone call was from my son. He was about 30 years old then and I didn't boss his life anymore. After he had left home I decided to let him go and do what he could do. But for once he phoned to tell me where he was going. My wife received the call and she told him, "John, your father has died and they are here trying to resuscitate him." Immediately he began to phone doctors. One of them was Dr. Clarence Robinson, who called some other specialists, and they began to prepare to receive me in the hospital. You see, God is an absolute perfectionist. He knows exactly what he is doing.

Meanwhile, the paramedics were working on my body. They would slow down a bit and my wife would say, "Oh no, he's not going to die! You keep working on him." About three months after this happened, I went down to the fire department and introduced myself to the chief paramedic.

He said, "Oh, you're the preacher who lives around here."
He shook my hand and told me, "Reverend, I want to tell
you something. You were as dead as any man I have ever
seen. But your wife wouldn't let you go. Just to appease her
I put saline in your veins. They were already collapsed and
I knew it was hopeless, but you don't know how insistent
she was!" I guess he thought he was telling me something
I didn't already know. The devil himself knows better than
to tangle with my wife!

They worked on me for about 40 minutes and they
finally got my heart to fibrillate, so they said, "We must get
him to the hospital immediately." The hospital I used was
about 12 miles away. They told my wife I would never live
that long, so they rushed me to a closer hospital, about four
miles away, and got me hooked up on the life support
machines. I remained on those machines, comatose, for
two weeks.

The long corridor with the beautiful light

I want to tell you what happened while I was comatose,
because it will be an encouragement to you that have loved
ones that have gone on to meet the Lord. How precious in
the sight of the Lord is the death of one of his saints. I can
tell you that from experience. It is precious in his sight.

I realized I was in the hospital, but I was not in my body.
I was in the hospital room, but while my body was lying in
the bed, I was up where the ceiling and the wall come
together at right angles. I could look down in every direction
at once. I could see the nurses come in and out of the room.
I looked out toward my left and saw a long corridor. Now
there was not a long corridor in that hospital. But I saw
this long corridor, and at the end of it was a beautiful little
light about the size of a beebee, so bright it would knock
your eyes out.

That light was so beautiful. I have been splashing paint
on canvas for years and I love to work with bright colors.

But I have never in my life witnessed colors as beautiful as when I died. I can't define the colors, I can't describe them. They were so beautiful they're unexplainable.

Then, as I was looking down in my hospital room, all of a sudden I went into this ecstasy of love. I can't begin to compare it to the emotion of love we experience in our physical bodies. I love my wife. We are about to celebrate our 104th wedding anniversary—52 for her and 52 for me. (Wait 'til I get home!) But on a scale of 1 to 10, my love for her is about a 5 compared to what I experienced when I died.

I love my wife, my children and my grandchildren, and I tell them so often. I think that's what we ought to do. I'm trying to love them so much that someday I'll register a 6. But let me tell you, when you leave this life to be with your loving Lord, you'll ring the bell at 10. That glorious ecstasy will thrill your being. You will be filled with the glory of his presence.

As I looked down that long corridor, I was waiting for someone to tell me to come in. I knew that the decision was being made whether I would go through that corridor or not. The third day I was in the hospital, the district superintendent, James Dodd, and another brother came to pray for me. My body was in that hospital bed with my eyes taped shut, but I saw them come into the room and go over to my bed to pray for me. They stood there and said, "Brother Hagee, we are here to pray for you." I was saying how glad I was to see them, but they paid no attention to me!

Months later, I told my wife one day, "Wasn't it wonderful for Brother Dodd and Brother Watkins to come pray for me?" She said, "You couldn't know that, you were in a coma. Your eyes were taped shut because they were turned back in your head." But I could tell her where they stood, what they were wearing, and repeat the prayer they prayed for me.

From a "flatliner" to a "carrot"

Well, I had been in the hospital for 48 hours and I was a "flatliner." My EEG showed nothing but a flat line. There was no brain activity whatsoever. The doctors told my family they should "pull the plug" and let me die peacefully. They said they could keep me alive mechanically, but I would never be anything but a vegetable because I was brain dead.

About that time, my son and my daughter remembered what I had told them when I went to see my oldest brother after he had a severe stroke. I went to see him before he went to be with the Lord. I told my children after that, "If I'm ever in that condition, you go get my cassette tapes out of my study and every day, whether I can talk to you or not, you play the New Testament in my ear. If you don't do anything else, I want you to put the word of God in my ears."

When they remembered what I had said, they went to my study and got my tapes. They put a tape recorder up in the hospital bed with me and began to play the word of God in my ears, like I had asked them. After 24 hours, the neurologist called my son into the room. He asked my son, "Mr. Hagee, do you see this bottom line?" John said he did. The brain wave was not a straight line any more. It was only a little blip, but it was no longer a flat line.

"This little line that's wiggling, that is about as much electricity as a carrot has in it," the doctor told my son. Not a great prognosis, but at least it was a vegetable with a name! The doctor didn't understand it and he couldn't explain it, but he said, "Your father is hearing what you are playing on that tape recorder. Whatever it is, it's bringing him back."

Now this was no Johnny-come-lately doctor, he is a highly respected neurologist. He later told me I had ruined his 40 years of practice by going 180° from everything he predicted. Well it wasn't me, it was the Lord. The reason I responded to that cassette tape of the scriptures was that the word of God was already in me. Don't think you can get sick and then go grab the word and believe for a miracle. Get charged up and full of the word now!

The word of God brought me back from the dead. They say when your brain is dead, it's dead. That is not so, and I refute it in the name of Jesus. It would be a greater miracle if my brain was dead—because that means he made me a new one and filled it with everything I ever knew. Now that's a miracle!

Well, I was in the hospital about 28 days. In that time I went from 210 pounds to 170 pounds. I literally melted because of the insult to my central nervous system. After about 20 days they let me stand up and walk a little. I went over to the mirror, and a living idiot was looking back at me. I saw a creature with eyes that looked dead, no expression on my face. And I had already progressed some by that time!

God strengthened my body and I went home from the hospital. They were giving me IQ tests and the results were terrible. Things that should take four minutes took me almost half an hour. I had to think in order to think. I groped for words and I couldn't put a sentence together. It was just gone. But God knew that he would make a new man with a new testimony of his glory and power. He gave me a new body by his spirit, as well as a new mind. It's been over ten years, and here I stand as his testimony.

The devil is in a pickle

The doctors had written a sad, gloomy letter to Social Security telling them that at best I'd be a babbling idiot, and at worst, a vegetable. Everybody was always talking about vegetables around me! The only person I know who is a vegetable is the devil, because he's in a pickle. Somebody told me a pickle isn't a vegetable, but I've got news for them. A pickle is a vegetable that has become what it is by the will of another. And our Lord has pickled the devil!

Well, when I got ready to retire, I passed all the tests Social Security tried to give me. I scored real high for a former carrot! I don't have to have anyone help me with my business. And I can discuss the scriptures with you until you can't stand it any longer. Turn me loose and a thirty minute sermon becomes an hour and a half. I'm back! And Jesus brought me back! He gave me all this for his glory. Hallelujah! Praise the Lord with me.

Chapter 9

Healing Scriptures

Pastor Hagee has recorded a cassette tape of healing scriptures. The foundation scriptures for the teaching on divine healing are listed below, along with Pastor Hagee's prayer from the Healing Scriptures tape.

I want to welcome you to the Healing Scriptures. We've been having a miracle explosion at Cornerstone Church and that miracle explosion has been initiated by the word of God. The Word is alive. It is sharper than any two-edged sword. The word of God is milk for spiritual infants. It is meat for men. It is the light of God in a dark world. It is the power that releases the anointing of the Lord Jesus Christ into your life.

The word of God is the basis of every healing and every miracle. Psalm 107:20 says, "He sent forth his word and healed them." The Bible says, "Have faith in God...Nothing is impossible to those who believe...Faith cometh by hearing, and hearing by the word of God."

I want you to hear this confession, and I want you to learn to speak it, because in the speaking of the word of God you release into your life the electrifying power that raised Jesus from the grave.

This is the confession:

Father, in the name of Jesus, I confess your word concerning healing. As I do this, I believe and say that your word will not return void, but will accomplish what it says it will. Therefore I believe in the name of Jesus that I am being healed as I hear the word of God. It is written in your word that Jesus himself took our infirmities and bore our sicknesses, therefore with great boldness and confidence I say on the authority of the written word of God that I am redeemed from the curse of sickness and I refuse to tolerate its symptoms.

Satan, I speak to you in the name of Jesus and say that your principalities and powers, your spirits of darkness and your spiritual wickedness in heavenly places are bound from operating against me in any way. I am the property of the Lord Jesus Christ. I am a child of God and I give you no place in me. I dwell in the secret place of the Most High God. I abide, I remain stable and fixed under the shadow of the Almighty. His power is in me and no foe can withstand me.

Now, Father, because I reverence and worship you, I have the assurance of your word that the angel of the Lord encamps round about me and delivers me from every evil work. No evil shall befall me. No plague nor calamity shall come near my dwelling. I confess that the word of God abides in me and produces in me perfect soundness of mind and wholeness in body and spirit, from the deepest parts of my nature in my immortal spirit, even to the joints and marrow of my bones. That word of God is medication and life to my flesh, for the law of the spirit of life operates in me and makes me free from the law of sin and death.

I have on the whole armor of God and the shield of faith protects me from all the fiery darts of the wicked one. Jesus is my high priest who hears my confession and I hold fast to this confession of faith through the word of God. I stand immovable and fixed and in full assurance that I have health and healing in the name of the Lord Jesus Christ, that my healing has been purchased through the blood of Jesus Christ and that as I hear these healing scriptures, the anointing power of the Lord is being released into my life to bring me divine health.

Exodus 15:26

If you listen carefully to the voice of the Lord your God and do what is right in his eyes, if you pay attention to his commands and keep all his decrees, I will not bring on you any of the diseases I brought on the Egyptians, for I am the Lord, who heals you.

Deuteronomy 7:15

The Lord will keep you free from every disease. He will not inflict on you the horrible diseases you knew in Egypt, but he will inflict them on all who hate you.

Deuteronomy 30:19-20

This day I call heaven and earth as witnesses against you that I have set before you life and death, blessings and curses. Now choose life, so that you and your children may live and that you may love the Lord you God, listen to his voice, and hold fast to him. For the Lord is your life.

Deuteronomy 32:39

See now that I myself am He! There is no god besides me. I put to death and I bring to life, I have wounded and I will heal, and no one can deliver out of my hand.

2 Kings 20:1-6

In those days Hezekiah became ill and was at the point of death. The prophet Isaiah son of Amoz went to him and said, "This is what the Lord says: Put your house in order, because you are going to die; you will not recover." Hezekiah turned his face to the wall and prayed to the Lord, "Remember, O Lord, how I have walked before you faithfully and with wholehearted devotion and have done what is good in your eyes." And Hezekiah wept bitterly.

Before Isaiah had left the middle court, the word of the Lord came to him: "Go back and tell Hezekiah, the leader of my people, 'This is what the Lord, the God of your father David, says: I have heard your prayer and seen your tears; I will heal you...I will add fifteen years to your life."

Psalm 6:2

Be merciful to me, Lord, for I am faint; O Lord, heal me, for my bones are in agony.

Psalm 30:2

O Lord my God, I called to you for help and you healed me.

Psalm 103:1-3

Praise the Lord, O my soul; all my inmost being, praise his holy name. Praise the Lord, O my soul, and forget not all his benefits—who forgives all your sins and heals all your diseases.

Psalm 107:20

He sent forth his word and healed them; he rescued them from the grave.

Psalm 147:3

He heals the brokenhearted and binds up their wounds.

Proverbs 3:5-8

Trust in the Lord with all your heart and lean not on your own understanding; in all your ways acknowledge him, and he will make your paths straight. Do not be wise in your own eyes; fear the Lord and shun evil. This will bring health to your body and nourishment to your bones.

Proverbs 4:20-22

My son, pay attention to what I say; listen closely to my words. Do not let them out of your sight, keep them within your heart; for they are life to those who find them and health to a man's whole body.

Proverbs 15:30

A cheerful look brings joy to the heart, and good news gives health to the bones.

Proverbs 16:24

Pleasant words are a honeycomb, sweet to the soul and healing to the bones.

Isaiah 38:16 [Hezekiah's testimony]

Lord, by such things men live; and my spirit finds life in them too. You restored me to health and let me live.

Isaiah 53:4-5

Surely he took up our infirmities and carried our sorrows, yet we considered him stricken by God, smitten by him, and afflicted. But he was pierced for our transgressions, he was crushed for our iniquities; the punishment that brought us peace was upon him, and by his wounds we are healed.

Isaiah 58:6-9

"Is not this the kind of fasting I have chosen: to loose the chains of injustice and untie the cords of the yoke, to set the oppressed free and break every yoke? Is it not to share your food with the hungry and to provide the poor wanderer with shelter—when you see the naked, to clothe him, and not to turn away from your own flesh and blood? Then your light will break forth like the dawn, and your healing with quickly appear; then your righteousness will go before you, and the glory of the Lord will be your rear guard. Then you will call, and the Lord will answer; you will cry for help and he will say: Here am I."

Jeremiah 30:17

But I will restore you to health and heal your wounds, declares the Lord.

Jeremiah 33:6

Nevertheless, I will bring health and healing to it; I will heal my people and will let them enjoy abundant peace and security.

Malachi 4:2

But for you who revere my name, the sun of righteousness will rise with healing in his wings.

Matthew 4:23-24

Jesus went throughout Galilee, teaching in their synagogues, preaching the good news of the kingdom, and healing every disease and sickness among the people. News about him spread all over Syria, and people brought to him all who were ill with various diseases, those suffering severe pain, the demon-possessed, those having seizures, and the paralyzed, and he healed them.

Matthew 8:2-3

A man with leprosy came and knelt before him and said, "Lord, if you are willing, you can make me clean." Jesus reached out his hand and touched the man. "I am willing," he said. "Be clean!" Immediately he was cured of his leprosy.

Matthew 8:5-10, 13

When Jesus had entered Capernaum, a centurion came to him, asking for help. "Lord," he said, "my servant lies at home paralyzed and in terrible suffering." Jesus said to him, "I will go and heal him." The centurion replied, "Lord, I do not deserve to have you come under my roof. But just say the word, and my servant will be healed. For I myself am a man under authority, with soldiers under me. I tell this one, 'Go,' and he goes; and that one, 'Come,' and he comes. I say to my servant, 'Do this,' and he does it."

When Jesus heard this, he was astonished and said to those following him, "I tell you the truth, I have not found anyone in Israel with such great faith...Then Jesus said to the centurion, "Go!" It will be done just as you believed it would." And his servant was healed at that very hour.

Matthew 8:14-17

When Jesus came into Peter's house, he saw Peter's mother-in-law lying in bed with a fever. He touched her hand and the fever left her, and she got up and began to wait on him.

When evening came, many who were demon-possessed were brought to him, and he drove out the spirits with a word and healed all the sick. This was to fulfill what was spoken through the prophet Isaiah: "He took up our infirmities and carried our diseases."

Matthew 9:27-29

As Jesus went on from there, two blind men followed him, calling out, "Have mercy on us, Son of David!" When he had gone indoors, the blind men came to him, and he asked them, "Do you believe that I am able to do this?" "Yes, Lord," they replied. Then he touched their eyes and said, "According to your faith will it be done to you;" and their sight was restored.

Matthew 9:35

Jesus went through all the towns and villages, teaching in their synagogues, preaching the good news of the kingdom and healing every disease and sickness.

Matthew 10:1, 8

He called his twelve disciples to him and gave them authority to drive out evil spirits and to heal every disease and sickness…"Heal the sick, raise the dead, cleanse those who have leprosy, drive out demons. Freely you have received, freely give."

Matthew 12:22

Then they brought him a demon-possessed man who was blind and mute, and Jesus healed him, so that he could both talk and see.

Matthew 14:35-36

And when the men of that place recognized Jesus, they sent word to all the surrounding country. People brought all their sick to him and begged him to let the sick just touch the edge of his cloak, and all who touched him were healed.

Matthew 15:30

Great crowds came to him, bringing the lame, the blind, the crippled, the mute and many others, and laid them at his feet; and he healed them.

Matthew 20:29-34

As Jesus and his disciples were leaving Jericho, a large crowd followed him. Two blind men were sitting by the roadside, and when they heard that Jesus was going by, they shouted, "Lord, Son of David, have mercy on us!" The crowd rebuked them and told them to be quiet, but they shouted all the louder, "Lord, Son of David, have mercy on us!"

Jesus stopped and called them, "What do you want me to do for you?" he asked. "Lord," they answered, "we want our sight." Jesus had compassion on them and touched their eyes. Immediately they received their sight and followed him.

Matthew 21:14

The blind and the lame came to him at the temple, and he healed them.

Mark 6:7, 12-13

Calling the Twelve to him, he sent them out two by two and gave them authority over evil spirits...They went out and preached that people should repent. They drove out many demons and anointed many sick people with oil and healed them.

Mark 6:56

And wherever he went—into villages, towns or countryside—they placed the sick in the marketplaces. They begged him to let them touch even the edge of his cloak, and all who touched him were healed.

Mark 16:17-18

"And these signs will accompany those who believe: In my name they will drive out demons; they will speak in new tongues; they will pick up snakes with their hands; and when they drink deadly poison, it will not hurt them at all; they will place their hands on sick people, and they will get well."

Luke 4:18-19, quoting *Isaiah 61:1-2*

"The spirit of the Lord is on me, because he has anointed me to preach good news to the poor. He has sent me to proclaim freedom for the prisoners and recovery of sight for the blind, to release the oppressed, to proclaim the year of the Lord's favor."

Luke 4:40

When the sun was setting, the people brought to Jesus all who had various kinds of sickness, and laying his hands on each one, he healed them.

Luke 5:15, 17

Yet the news about him spread all the more, so that crowds of people came to hear him and to be healed of their sicknesses...One day he was teaching...and the power of the Lord was present for him to heal the sick.

Luke 6:17-19

He went down with them and stood on a level place. A large crowd of his disciples was there and a great number of people from all over Judea, from Jerusalem, and from the coast of Tyre and Sidon, who had come to hear him and to be healed of their diseases. Those troubled by evil spirits were cured, and the people all tried to touch him, because power was coming from him and healing them all.

Luke 8:41-55

Then a man named Jairus, a ruler of the synagogue, came and fell at Jesus' feet, pleading with him to come to his house because his only daughter, a girl of about twelve, was dying. As Jesus was on his way, the crowds almost crushed him. And a woman was there who had been subject to bleeding for twelve years, but no one could heal her. She came up behind him and touched the edge of his cloak, and immediately her bleeding stopped.

"Who touched me?" Jesus asked. When they all denied it, Peter said, "Master, the people are crowding and pressing against you." But Jesus said, "Someone touched me; I know that power has gone out from me." Then the woman, seeing that she could not go unnoticed, came trembling and fell at his feet. In the presence of all the people, she told why she had touched him and how she had been instantly healed. Then he said to her, "Daughter, your faith has healed you. Go in peace."

While Jesus was still speaking, someone came from the house of Jairus, the synagogue ruler. "Your daughter is dead," he said. "Don't bother the teacher any more." Hearing this, Jesus said to Jairus, "Don't be afraid; just believe, and she will be healed." When he arrived at the house of Jairus, he did not let anyone go in with him except Peter, John and James, and the child's father and mother.

Meanwhile, all the people were wailing and mourning for her. "Stop wailing," Jesus said. "She is not dead but asleep." They laughed at him, knowing that she was dead. But he took her by the hand and said, "My child, get up!" Her spirit returned, and at once she stood up. Then Jesus told them to give her something to eat.

Luke 9:11

He welcomed [the crowds] and spoke to them about the kingdom of God, and healed those who needed healing.

Luke 13:10-13

On a Sabbath Jesus was teaching in one of the synagogues, and a woman was there who had ben crippled by a spirit for eighteen years. She was bent over and could not straighten up at all. When Jesus saw her, he called her forward and said to her, "Woman, you are set free from your infirmity." Then he put his hands on her, and immediately she straightened up and praised God.

Luke 17:12-14

As [Jesus] was going into a village, ten men who had leprosy met him. They stood at a distance and called out in a loud voice, "Jesus, Master, have pity on us!" When he saw them he said, "Go show yourselves to the priest." And as they went, they were cleansed.

John 4:46-53

Once more he visited Cana in Galilee, where he had turned the water into wine. And there was a certain royal official whose son lay sick at Capernaum. When this man heard that Jesus had arrived in Galilee from Judea, he went to him and begged him to come and heal his son, who was close to death...The royal official said, "Sir, come down before my child dies." Jesus replied, "You may go. Your son will live."

The man took Jesus at his word and departed. While he was still on the way, his servants met him with the news that his boy was living. When he inquired as to the time when his son got better, they said to him, "The fever left him yesterday at the seventh hour." Then the father realized that this was the exact time at which Jesus had said to him, "Your son will live."

John 5:2-9

Now there is in Jerusalem near the Sheep Gate a pool, which in Aramaic is called Bethesda and which is surrounded by five covered colonnades. Here a great number of disabled people used to lie—the blind, the lame, the paralyzed. One who was there had been an invalid for thirty-eight years.

When Jesus saw him lying there and learned that he had been in this condition for a long time, he asked him, "Do you want to get well?" "Sir," the invalid replied, "I have no one to help me into the pool when the water is stirred. While I am trying to get in, someone else goes down ahead of me." Then Jesus said to him, "Get up! Pick up your mat and walk." At once the man was cured; he picked up his mat and walked.

Acts 3:2-8

Now a man crippled from birth was being carried to the temple gate called Beautiful, where he was put every day to beg from those going into the temple courts. When he saw Peter and John about to enter, he asked them for money.

Peter looked straight at him, as did John. Then Peter said, "Look at us!" So the man gave them his attention, expecting to get something from them. Then Peter said, "Silver or gold I do not have, but what I have I give you. In the name of Jesus Christ of Nazareth, walk."

Taking him by the right hand, he helped him up,

and instantly the man's feet and ankles became strong. He jumped to his feet and began to walk. Then he went with them into the temple courts, walking and jumping, and praising God.

Acts 5:12, 15-16

The apostles performed many miraculous signs and wonders among the people...As a result, people brought the sick into the streets and laid them on beds and mats so that at least Peter's shadow might fall on some of them as he passed by. Crowds gathered also from the towns around Jerusalem, bringing their sick and those tormented by evil spirits, and all of them were healed.

Acts 8:6-7

When the crowds heard Philip and saw the miraculous signs he did, they all paid close attention to what he said. With shrieks, evil spirits came out of many, and many paralytics and cripples were healed.

Acts 9:32-35

As Peter traveled about the country, he went to visit the saints in Lydda. There he found a man named Aeneas, a paralytic who had been bedridden for eight years. "Aeneas," Peter said to him, "Jesus Christ heals you. Get up and take care of your mat." Immediately Aeneas got up. All those who lived in Lydda and Sharon saw him and turned to the Lord.

Acts 10:38

[You know] how God anointed Jesus of Nazareth with the Holy Spirit and power, and how he went around doing good and healing all who were under the power of the devil, because God was with him.

Acts 14:8-10

In Lystra there sat a man crippled in his feet, who was lame from birth and had never walked. He listened to

Paul as he was speaking. Paul looked directly at him, saw that he had faith to be healed and called out, "Stand up on your feet!" At that, the man jumped up and began to walk.

Acts 28:7-9

There was an estate nearby that belonged to Publius, the chief official of the island...His father was sick in bed, suffering from fever and dysentery. Paul went in to see him and, after prayer, placed his hands on him and healed him. When this had happened, the rest of the sick on the island came and were cured.

Romans 8:11

And if the Spirit of him who raised Jesus from the dead is living in you, he who raised Christ from the dead will also give life to your mortal bodies through his Spirit, who lives in you.

1 Corinthians 11:27, 29-30

Therefore, whoever eats the bread or drinks the cup of the Lord in an unworthy manner will be guilty of sinning against the body and blood of the Lord...For anyone who eats and drinks without recognizing the body of the Lord eats and drinks judgment on himself. That is why many among you are weak and sick, and a number of you have fallen asleep.

1 Corinthians 12:8-10

To one there is given through the Spirit the message of wisdom, to another the message of knowledge by means of the same Spirit, to another faith by the same Spirit, to another gifts of healing by that one Spirit, to another miraculous powers...

1 Corinthians 12:28

And in the church God has appointed first of all apostles, second prophets, third teachers, then workers of miracles, also those having gifts of healing...

James 5:14-17

Is any one of you sick? He should call the elders of the church to pray over him and anoint him with oil in the name of the Lord. And the prayer offered in faith will make the sick person well; the Lord will raise him up. If he has sinned, he will be forgiven. Therefore confess your sins to each other and pray for each other so that you may be healed. The prayer of a righteous man is powerful and effective.

1 Peter 2:24

He himself bore our sins in his body on the tree, so that we might die to sins and live for righteousness; by his wounds you have been healed.

3 John 2

Dear friend, I pray that you may enjoy good health and that all may go well with you, even as your soul is getting along well.

The Power To Heal

This book was originally packaged with a cassette tape of Healing Scriptures recorded by Pastor John Hagee and a cassette tape with the testimony of Lizzy Gross's healing.
Call or write to order additional copies.

The Power to Heal package includes
The Power to Heal (book)
Healing Scriptures (tape)
Lizzy's Miracle (tape)

O-3 .... $15.00

John Hagee Ministries
P.O. Box 1400
San Antonio, TX 78295

(512) 491-5100